Since time immemorial, men have assumed superior innate qualities which have justified them in exerting power over the other sex right up to the twentieth century. The last few years have seen the emergence of a new literary genre: to show that despite this, women have managed to become outstanding writers, artists, scientists, explorers, rulers and politicians. Of such books, none discusses a fundamental question: is the supposed male superiority biological, or has it arisen for some other reason over the course of time? This is the issue that *Androcentrism: The Ascendancy of Man* addresses.

The stronger physique of males may have given Palaeolithic man a feeling of superiority, but the two sexes probably lived in fairly gender-neutral, or even matriarchal, groups right up to the end of the Neolithic Age. Charles Pasternak argues that it was the emergence of hierarchies, like chiefdom, that largely sparked androcentrism. It became established as villages grew into towns, with the ownership of property as an important ingredient, during the Bronze Age. While the Mediaeval Period was a time of slight respite for women, the Age of Enlightenment in Europe did not bolster this trend; it reversed it. Not until the latter half of the nineteenth century was androcentrism beginning to be seriously questioned, but significant change happened only after World War I. Today androcentrism has virtually disappeared from most parts of the world. It was just a cultural blip, albeit one that lasted over 5,000 years.

Androcentrism

The Ascendancy of Man

Other World Scientific Titles by the Author

Biosciences 2000: Current Aspects and Prospects for the
Next Millennium
ISBN: 978-1-86094-195-5

Other Titles by the Author

Biochemistry of Differentiation
Radioimmunoassay and Related Topics in Clinical Biochemistry
An Introduction to Human Biochemistry
Monovalent Cations in Biological Systems
The Molecules Within Us: Our Body in Health and Disease
Quest: The Essence of Humanity
What Makes Us Human?
Access Not Excess: The Search for Better Nutrition
Blinkers: Scientific Ignorance and Evasion
Africa South of the Sahara: Continued Failure or Delayed Success?

Androcentrism

The Ascendancy of Man

Charles Pasternak

Oxford International Biomedical Centre, UK

World Scientific

NEW JERSEY · LONDON · SINGAPORE · BEIJING · SHANGHAI · HONG KONG · TAIPEI · CHENNAI · TOKYO

Published by

World Scientific Publishing Co. Pte. Ltd.

5 Toh Tuck Link, Singapore 596224

USA office: 27 Warren Street, Suite 401-402, Hackensack, NJ 07601

UK office: 57 Shelton Street, Covent Garden, London WC2H 9HE

Library of Congress Cataloging-in-Publication Data
Names: Pasternak, Charles A. (Charles Alexander), author.
Title: Androcentrism : the ascendancy of man / Charles Pasternak,
    Oxford International Biomedical Centre, UK.
Description: New Jersey : World Scientific, [2022] |
    Includes bibliographical references and index.
Identifiers: LCCN 2021029483 | ISBN 9789811240836 (hardcover) |
    ISBN 9789811241840 (paperback) | ISBN 9789811240843 (ebook) |
    ISBN 9789811240850 (ebook other)
Subjects: LCSH: Androcentrism. | Men--Social conditions.
Classification: LCC HQ1090 .P387 2022 | DDC 305.31--dc23
LC record available at https://lccn.loc.gov/2021029483

British Library Cataloguing-in-Publication Data
A catalogue record for this book is available from the British Library.

For any available supplementary material, please visit
https://www.worldscientific.com/worldscibooks/10.1142/12384#t=suppl

Desk Editor: Shaun Tan Yi Jie

Typeset by Stallion Press
Email: enquiries@stallionpress.com

Printed in Singapore

To the memory of the millions of women throughout the world and across the ages whose lives have been constrained by male dominance.

Acknowledgements

This book owes its appearance to a deadly disease: the Covid-19 pandemic that hit Europe in the spring of 2020. I was locked down in London, unable to go to my office (the Oxford International Biomedical Centre at Culham), just outside Oxford. I equipped myself with Andrew Roberts' *Churchill* and Simon Heffer's *High Minds* (nigh on 2,000 pages between them) but was rapidly approaching their end. What to do? I would write another book.

I am grateful for advice, information, comments and support from Mary Beard, Sarah-Jane Blakemore, Christopher Boehm, Alan Bond, John Brooke, Catherine Dulac, Clare Enders, Patricia Fara, Iris Gruenebaum, Christopher Kennard, Richard Langworth, Diane LeBow, Kasia Lewis, Roger Lewis, Henrietta Leyser, Christopher Millar, Teresa Milner, Anna Pasternak, Robert Plomin, Aridea Fezzi Price, Gina Rippon, Andrew Roberts, Andrew Robinson, Chris Stringer and Andrew Wallas. I am indebted to the staff of the London Library for their continuous assistance, and especially to Simon Hoar who suggested relevant articles that I could access online during the brief time when I could not borrow books from that excellent institution. A special thanks to Shaun Tan Yi Jie, my forbearing editor at World Scientific.

About the Author

Professor Charles Pasternak is a British biochemist and founding Director of the Oxford International Biomedical Centre, of which he is currently President. He has published over 250 original papers and reviews, and is the founding Editor-in-Chief of *Bioscience Reports*, helming the journal for 28 years. He is also the editor of *Biosciences 2000* (World Scientific, 1999), and author of seven other books.

Educated at Oxford University, Charles Pasternak spent 15 years on the staff of the Oxford Biochemistry Department, during which time he also held a teaching Fellowship at Worcester College, Oxford. He spent two years as a Post-Doctoral Fellow in the Pharmacology Department of Yale University Medical School, and subsequently held an Eleanor Roosevelt Fellowship of the International Union Against Cancer in the Department of Neurosciences at the University of California San Diego Medical School in La Jolla. In 1976 he was invited to move to St. George's Hospital Medical School, University of London, in order to set up a new Department of Biochemistry, which he subsequently expanded into a larger Department of Cellular and Molecular Sciences as Founder-Chairman. He is currently President of the Oxford International Biomedical Centre which he founded in 1992.

Charles Pasternak is a tireless promoter of international scientific collaboration. He has been a member of the Executive Committee for a UNESCO initiative on Molecular and Cellular Biology, a member of the Education Committee of the International Union of Biochemistry and

Molecular Biology (IUBMB), a member of the International Advisory Board for the Chulabhorn Research Institute, Bangkok and a member of the Scientific Board of Antenna Technologie, Geneva. In 1979 he founded the Cell Surface Research Fund in order to foster international research links and scientific meetings on various aspects of fundamental and clinical research on the cell surface. In 1993 he received the degree of Doctor Honoris Causa and Palade medal from the University of Bucharest, in 1995 the honour of Amigo de Venezuela from the Fundacion Venezuela Positiva, and in 2002 was elected Foreign Member of the Polish Academy of Arts and Sciences.

Contents

Prologue

Christmas 2018. In the picturesque village of Saanen, the bell of the Mauritsiuskirche tolls. At an altitude of 1,000 metres, high above Montreux on Lake Geneva, the air is fresh and crisp. Snow is on the way. I am chatting to my hostess, Swedish-American Professor of History at the City University of New York. Helena asks me what I am writing about at the moment. I explain my project of describing outstanding females through the ages and across the globe in order to show that the intellectual capability of a woman is the same as that of a man. She considers this insulting and unnecessary in today's world. I subsequently dropped the project — not because of Helena's views but because the subject was being crowded out by others. In fact a new literary genre had appeared: to describe the lives of women who have managed to become outstanding writers, artists, scientists, explorers, rulers and politicians. Jenni Murray's *A History of Britain in 21 Women*, followed by *A History of the World in 21 Women* [1] are examples. Another is Marilyn French's *From Eve to Dawn, a History of Women in the World* [2]. Of such books, none addresses a fundamental question: is the supposed male superiority innate or has it arisen for some other reason over the course of time? This is the issue I now address.

160 years ago, in Hartford, Connecticut was born a girl called Charlotte. Her father was a librarian and distant relative of Harriet Beecher Stowe. She herself would become a well-known author (to 19th-century Americans if not to my contemporary readers) for works such as *Herland*, a mythical country occupied solely by women. She has been called — alongside William Morris — 'one of four late 19th-century visionaries'. She was

Charlotte Perkins Gilman and she coined the word androcentric [3] from Greek, meaning 'man-centred'. I have used the corresponding noun, in preference to the wider-meaning word 'patriarchy', to indicate the central theme of this book: men's perceived superiority over women. The subtitle, adherents of political correctness will be pleased to note, refers to 'man' in the sense of masculine, not as Jacob Bronowski did in his 1973 book and TV documentary entitled *The Ascent of Man*, in the sense of 'human'. What I am suggesting is that from late Neolithic times on — the start point for Bronowski's account of human achievements over the last ten millennia — men began to exercise control over women. I could easily have called this book 'The Descent of Woman'.

By the 19th century men realised that Man the Hunter versus Woman the Gatherer was insufficient to justify their perceived superiority. Brain was added to brawn. But muscular strength does not affect the brain. Perhaps, then, a heightened empathy in women — engendered through child-bearing — compromises their ability to take hard decisions in stressful situations? Is there, then, a 'female' as opposed to a 'male' brain? Some scientists seem to think so. But extensive research has failed to support such a view. The 'female' brain does not exist. My friend Helena, and others like her, are justified in feeling insulted at the very suggestion (chapter 1).

If much of androcentrism cannot be explained in biological terms, it must be cultural rather than innate. If so, when did it arise? Archaeological evidence suggests that right up to the Neolithic Age, small communities lived in relatively gender-neutral societies; some were actually matriarchal. The advent of agriculture 12,000 years ago sowed the seeds of androcentrism (pun intended). For with the planting and harvesting of crops came the domestication of sheep and cattle. These are easier to steal than crops, and herders took on extra authority that led to the emergence of chiefs. 'Chiefs first appeared in the archaeological record of the Pontic Caspian steppes', the region to the north of the Black and Caspian Seas, from the mouth of the Dniester in the west to that of the Ural River in the east, 'when domesticated cattle, sheep and goats first became widespread' [4], some 7,000 years ago. Chiefs were undeniably male and bossy.

The people of the Pontic Caspian steppes, also known as Kurgan, did more than herd cattle. They tamed the wild horse that originated in Mongolia. They invented, or acquired from eastern Europe or Mesopotamia, the wheel. This led to a new form of transport: the wagon (or cart). All these activities were carried out by males and there seems no reason to doubt that Kurgan society was one of the birthplaces of androcentrism. From the 4th millennium BCE onwards, the Kurgan tribes began to migrate westwards into Europe and eastwards into Asia. The result? From the west coast of Ireland to the banks of the Brahmaputra male authority came to be accepted as a way of life (chapter 2).

In 1842 the young Friedrich Engels was sent by his father, a prosperous owner of textile mills in Barmen (today's Wuppertal) and Salford in England, to spend some time at his Salford factory. Friedrich had served in the artillery and studied in Berlin. There he had developed an interest in Hegelian philosophy, one result of which was a tendency towards atheism. Friedrich senior thought that a spell in his Salford plant would cure his son of such radical ideas. The result, of course, was the opposite. On the way to Salford the 22-year-old Friedrich stopped off at the offices of the *Rheinische Zeitung* in Cologne where he met Karl Marx, two years his senior.

The relevance of this as far as this book is concerned is not so much the development of Engels' collaboration with Marx, as the fact that he 'evolved a new synthesis which stressed emerging class differentiation and man's successful control of property and the surplus as the base both for the emergence of the state *and male patriarchal control*' (my italics) [5]. In other words it was the advent of social hierarchies towards the end of the Neolithic Age that spawned man's authority over women. By the time of the Bronze Age, androcentrism — surely the most extreme form of hierarchies — had infiltrated every civilisation that arose.

The earliest of these emerged in the city of Uruk, along the banks of the Euphrates in southern Mesopotamia, around 3000 BCE. Somewhat later another city, Ur, grew up further downstream. Together they formed the Sumerian empire. This was later absorbed into that of Babylon, a city upstream of Uruk and at one time probably the largest city in the world. Another civilisation grew up along the valley of the Indus around 2500 BCE. This developed out of two cities: Harappa in the north and Mohenjo-daro downstream in the south. The Harappa, as the people of the Indus Valley are known, traded extensively with the city states of Mesopotamia. Through this they absorbed some of their culture. But not, it seems, the practice of slavery that was endemic throughout all other civilisations. This is probably because the Harappa were less warlike and therefore acquired few prisoners. In other ways, too, the people of the Indus Valley were probably less androcentric than elsewhere. In Egypt the pharaonic civilisation developed contemporaneously with that of Uruk. Apart from royal women — wife, mother or daughter of the pharaoh — and associated elites, women had few roles. They could not even become scribes. Yet the legacy of Egypt, its pyramids and temples, has outlasted anything that Mesopotamia could throw up (chapter 3).

2,500 years ago, three of the world's greatest thinkers were born. In Greece Socrates expounded his philosophy of questioning all precepts by dialogue, which has become central to Western philosophy. In India Gautama Buddha founded a religion based on a life of spirituality, simplicity and peace. It is the only faith that is fairly gender-neutral and is today practised by over 500 million people worldwide. In China Confucius developed a philosophy that also prescribes leading a moral, just and peaceful life. In this case, however, male superiority is assumed. Not a religion but a way of life, Confucianism was strongly promoted by Mao Zedong, but no more than six million people are said to follow its precepts today.

Socrates, Gautama Buddha and Confucius lived during the early period of what has been called the Classical Age. Three influential cultures dominated the period that lasted until the 6th century CE: Persia, Greece and Rome. The Achaemenid Empire, founded by Cyrus the Great (*c* 600–530 BCE) was by far the largest nation of its day. It stretched from Afghanistan in the East across all of present-day Persia to Mesopotamia and Anatolia in the West. Although most women had few rights — as in Egypt they could not become scribes — 'ownership and control of estates showed the extent of economic independence enjoyed by Persian royal women' [6].

The relatively easier life open to aristocratic and other elite women is a recurring theme throughout history.

In Athens two classes of women lived side by side. The first were citizens. Their sole occupation was to marry and produce children. The second were foreigners, born outside the city. They were not citizens and could not marry an Athenian citizen. On the other hand their lives were not restricted to the household. They could attend social functions with Athenian men. Aspasia of Miletus, the wife of Pericles, 'boldly surpassed the limited expectations for women by establishing a renowned girl's school and a popular salon. She lived free of female seclusion and conducted herself like a male intellectual while expounding on current events, philosophy, and rhetoric' [7]. The philosopher Aristotle, on the other hand, 'viewed the creation of a female child as the unsuccessful attempt to generate a male' [8].

Roman women fell somewhere between these two categories. Like Greek citizens their first duty was to marry and have children. But they could also socialise with men, feast with them and discuss politics and poetry. Like Athenian women, though, they had no vote and could not participate in elections. On at least two occasions, however, women persuaded the Senate to change its mind. Both involved money. In 213 BCE a decree proposed that the amount of gold a woman could possess should be limited. The women caused an uproar and the Senate changed its mind. Another instance occurred a little under 200 years later, when the cash-strapped Senate proposed that over a thousand of the richest women should help to support the Republic. Once more, feminine argument won the day [9]. Nevertheless, 'one earnest Roman anthologist of the first century AD was able to rake up just three examples of women whose natural condition did not manage to keep them silent in the forum' [10].

The history of the Romans produced two women of determination and courage who were able to cause the leadership a good deal of trouble. The first was Boudica, the Queen of the Iceni. In around 60 CE she led an insurrection against the occupiers of Britain. Her campaign caused much bloodshed but eventually failed. The second was Zenobia, Queen of Palmyra in Syria. In *c* 268 CE she launched her army against the Roman occupiers of the eastern Mediterranean. She successfully took the province of Egypt. But when a series of weak emperors was succeeded by the assertive Aurelian, her luck ran out. She was defeated and carried to Rome in chains (or committed suicide on the way) (chapter 4).

The Middle Ages, roughly from 500 to 1500, were a period of relative easing for women. Not all historians, however, subscribe to such a view. The main reason for women's increased independence during this time can, I believe, be ascribed to the rise of Christianity. First because the religion itself, as presented in the Gospels of the New Testament, includes two women as key players: Mary the mother of Jesus and Mary the Magdalene. Second because convents under different religious orders sprang up in Europe from the 5th century onwards. These allowed women to escape an unwanted marriage in exchange for a vow of chastity and a spiritual life free from male interference. More than that, they gave many the opportunity to realise their innate potential in a number of ways. Hildegard von Bingen, the nuns of Helfta (also in Germany), Marie de France, Birgitta of Sweden, Julian of Norwich and Christine de Pizan are examples.

During Anglo-Saxon times, as the name suggests, England was a divided country until the 11th century. The south and southwest (Wessex) of England, as well as the west Midlands (English Mercia), were in English hands. The east Midlands (Danish Mercia) and further north beyond York were in territory occupied by the Danes. They represented those Vikings who would eventually integrate into the population. After the Norman Conquest of 1066 England became a single nation, while France now entered a period during which its people were divided. To the west were the lands occupied by the Normans, which became known as Angevine during the reign of Henry II — Count of Anjou (hence Angevin) — in the 12th century. They stretched from Normandy in the north, along the coast to Aquitaine in the south. To the east, from the English Channel in the north to the Mediterranean in the south, was the country of the Capets who were descendants of Charlemagne. Not until the end of the Hundred Years War (1337–1453) would the Capets become sole rulers of France.

The Medieval period saw several women of fortitude whose independence of action has given them a place in history. Three of them are linked to the regions I have just described. Aethelflaed was the eldest daughter of the English king Alfred and known as the Lady of Mercia. She took land from the Danes in England and prevented several invasions by Vikings from the continent. Eleanor of Aquitaine was probably unique in marrying first a king of France (Louis VII) and then a king of England (the future Henry II, 11 years her junior whom she outlived by 15 years). Joan of Arc was a peasant girl with visions and apparent second sight who, remarkably, was integral to the defeat of the English by the French and thus bringing to an end the Hundred Years War (chapter 5).

By the 16th century the demographic map of Europe looked much the same as it does today, with three exceptions. The German-speaking states, like Prussia, Hanover, Bavaria and so on, would not be unified until 1871. At precisely this date the Italian states, such as Venice, Milan, Papal States, Naples and so forth, became once more a single nation as it had been under the Romans. In contrast the multilingual lands of the vast Hapsburg empire were split into separate nations in 1919. Whether state or nation, all of Europe (apart from Switzerland after 1648) was ruled by monarchs, and they were generally male. Four exceptional women, two in the 16th century and two in the 18th, bucked this trend. One was of Italian origin, one of English, and two of German. But they had four important traits in common that any androcentric man would recognise: fortitude (two overcame quite traumatic events in their childhood), ambition, determination (one of them used murder to achieve her aims) and a good intellect. But none was in any way androgyne. They fell in love with the opposite sex, produced 30 children between them, enjoyed dancing, wore extravagant clothes and sported costly jewellery. They were Catherine de Medici (1519–1589), Elizabeth I of England (1533–1603), Maria Theresa of Austria (1717–1780) and Catherine II of Russia (1729–1796).

One might have thought that the Enlightenment during the 17th and 18th century would have changed men's attitude towards women, but that would be wrong. Philosophers across Europe were expounding on liberty and freedom, a new nation founded on these precepts was born in America, and an old one adopted them to overthrow its monarchy. But androcentrism continued unabated. Not until the latter half of the 19th century were politicians induced to consider the enfranchisement of women (chapter 6).

By the time of the 20th century the suffragette movement throughout the world was in full swing. In many countries it resulted not just in women having the vote, but being able to stand for office themselves. Following World War II, politically prominent women were elected to leadership of their country. The first, in 1960, was Sirimavo Bandaranaike in Sri Lanka. She was followed in 1966 by Indira Gandhi in India, in 1969 by Golda Meir in Israel, in 1979 by Margaret Thatcher in the UK, in 1981 by Gro Harlem Brundtland in Norway, in 1986 by Corazon Aquino in the Philippines, in 1988 by Benazir Bhutto in Pakistan, in 1994 by Chandrika Kumaratunga in Sri Lanka, in 1997 by Jenny Shipley in New Zealand, in 2005 by Angela Merkel in Germany and in 2006 by Ellen Johnson Sirleaf in Liberia. 11 female leaders, none of whom attained office due to an accident of royal birth, in just over four decades.

In most countries, the Islamist Middle Eastern ones excepted, androcentrism is finally dead. Well, not quite. Pockets remain. In early 20th century Carinthia, for example, the mother of writer and Nobel laureate Peter Handke, 'was born into conditions comparable to serfdom. ... Her father allowed her an elementary schooling — no more than a daughter deserved. Women were condemned to pathetic, nugatory lives. At church fairs, fortune tellers read only the palms of boys; "a girl's future was a joke".' [11]. And in 1982, as the men were sipping their port at a dinner party in Downing Street, Margaret Thatcher could still say, 'Shall we join the ladies?' [12] (chapter 7).

If androcentrism arose only 5,000 or so years ago, its absence should be retained in isolated communities that continue to live in a primitive way, unaffected by the cultural and technological changes that occurred in their neighbouring societies. By the turn of the present century, there were still five million people living in various parts of the world who could be described as 'Indigenous Peoples Who Are or Were Hunter-Gatherers' [13]. Accounts of the lifestyles of these people by anthropologists and explorers vary, even in regard to the same community. This is not surprising as they were made over the span of more than 100 years, during which contact with 'modern' communities — that were themselves becoming more gender neutral — increased.

Nevertheless it is clear that in the small groups of indigenous people who have resisted the values of contemporary society, more egalitarian ways of living have endured. From the Bushmen of the Kalahari and the Hadza of Tanzania to the Aborigines of the Malay Peninsula (who are surprisingly both matriarchal and Muslim), from Australian Aborigines and Trobriand Islanders to the Hopi of North America, there is little evidence that the more androcentric ways of the rest of the world ever emerged. That surely supports the thrust of this book: that androcentrism is a cultural, not an innate, feature of *H sapiens* (chapter 8).

Notes

1. published by Oneworld in 2016 and 2018 respectively.
2. this was to have been a four-volume work. Vol 1, *From Prehistory to the First Millennium*, appeared in 2007. Sadly, French died two years later.
3. Robertson (2018), chapter 5: *Charlotte Perkins Gilman's Motherly Utopia*, pp 172–222; 'androcentric' mentioned on p 198.
4. Anthony (2007), p 160.
5. Gail Omvedt: *The Origin of Patriarchy*, a review of *The Creation of Patriarchy* by Gerda Lerner (1986) published in *Economic and Political Weekly*, October 31, 1987.
6. Brosius (1996), p 199.
7. *The Oxford Classical Dictionary* (1992).
8. Daniel T Kline: *Female Childhoods* in Dinshaw and Wallace (2003), p 14.
9. Donaldson (1907), pp 99 and 104 respectively.
10. Beard (2017), p 11.
11. taken from a review of Peter Handke's *A Sorrow Beyond Dreams* by Tanjil Rashid in the *Financial Times* of 6 Dec 2019.
12. from *The Journals of Kenneth Rose* (ed by D R Thorpe, vol 2; London: Weidenfeld and Nicolson, 2019), p 64.
13. Robert K Hitchcock and Megan Biesele: *Introduction*, in Schweitzer *et al* (2000), p 5.

Chapter 1

Genes and their Expression: The 'Female' Brain

'All the talk in the world will never shake the proposition that men are stronger than women in every shape. They have greater muscular and nervous force, greater intellectual force, greater vigour of character' [1]. These words were written by James Fitzjames Stephen (1829–1894), a respected lawyer, civil servant and High Court judge, for which he received a baronetcy. His *Liberty, Equality, Fraternity* published in 1873, from which I have just quoted, was considered to be the 'finest exposition of conservative thought in the latter half of the nineteenth century' [2]. Stephen's views were echoed by others of his time. Thus 'superiority is not a thing of man's devising, but of God's'. Moreover 'the female is by a law of nature put under the domination of the male' [3]. Even Charles Darwin thought that 'the chief distinction in the intellectual powers of the two sexes is shown by man's attaining to a higher eminence in whatever he takes up, than can woman — whether requiring deep thought, reason or imagination, or merely the use of the senses or the hands' [4].

On the other hand, the Principal of St Andrews University in Scotland, writing in 1907, thought that 'a true conception of woman's ideal life can be reached only by the long experience of many ages. The very first and most essential element in the harmonious development of woman's nature, as it is of man's, is freedom, but this is the very last thing which she acquires. Impediments have arisen on every hand to hinder her from bringing her powers into full activity. Ignorance, prejudice, absurd modes of thought prevalent in particular ages, conventional restraints of an arbitrary nature, laws that have sought to attain special aims without regard to general culture and well-being — these and like causes have prevented us from seeing what women might become if she were left unfettered by all influences but those that are benign and congenial' [5].

Who was right? The gist of this book is that it was the prescient Principal of St Andrews. Of course men have stronger muscles. On average males have 50% more skeletal muscle mass than females. The strength of their muscles also differs. According to a recent study, 'the skeletal muscles of men are faster and render higher maximum output compared to women's skeletal muscles. However, women have the advantage of recovering faster and being more fatigue-resistant. Estrogen-β (a hormone) seems to have an effect in muscle contractile speed, making men more efficient in producing power and women more efficient in healing' [6]. Of course, the person-to-person variation is huge. A strong well-built woman can outshine a weak puny man anytime. But as regards James Stephens' remark, there is no evidence that muscle strength affects the brain. I will come to Charles Darwin's remarks later in the chapter.

Men's muscular superiority has led to the view that Man the Hunter epitomises male supremacy. For ever since *Homo habilis*, an ancestor of *H sapiens*, discovered more than two million years ago how to fashion weapons made of stone or wood, males have hunted animals for meat. Females, it is assumed, largely gathered fruit and edible plants, and reared children. This continued for the next 1,990,000 or so years. Only during the last 0.5% of the time that *Homo* species have roamed the earth, have humans begun to live differently. Our brain, like the rest of our body, is shaped by Stone-Age living and has not changed significantly over the last 300,000 years, which is when *H sapiens* emerged. No wonder we make so many mistakes in looking after our planet. The last 10,000 years may have seen a staggering increase in our quality of life, the last hundred an exponential increase in novel technologies. But have we become any wiser? The 19th-century poet Alfred Tennyson got it right when he said 'knowledge comes, but wisdom lingers'.

Returning to Man the Hunter. Because hunting is more demanding than picking berries off trees, men came to be regarded as superior in other ways as well. Well into the 19th century, as I have illustrated, male leadership has been assumed to be inbred. But among (other) animals, hunting is not a particularly male characteristic. Female lions are better hunters than their male counterparts: they are superior at stalking, and are 30% faster when chasing their prey. Moreover, among the few remaining indigenous tribes who live by hunting and foraging, there is little evidence of any gender superiority. The Bushmen of the Kalahari for example, one of the longest surviving hunting communities, live in an essentially egalitarian society (chapter 8). Perhaps more closely related animals, like chimpanzees, offer a clue as to the assumed innate cause of androcentrism?

The DNA of humans and chimpanzees is more than 95% similar, in terms of the relative abundance of constituent nucleotides (A-T versus G-C pairs). The DNA of a male human resembles that of a male chimpanzee more than it does that of a female human (and *vice versa*). This is due to two reasons. First, because the genes of a human contain merely slight mutations in analogous genes in a chimpanzee. There is no such thing as a specifically 'human' or 'chimpanzee' gene, as scientists (including myself [7]) speculated 20 years ago. Sequencing the human and chimpanzee genomes (the entirety of their constituent genes) has proved the point. This, incidentally, confirms Darwin's theory of evolution by natural selection. Secondly, the Y chromosome (recall that males have a Y and an X chromosome, whereas females have two X chromosomes, the other 22 chromosomes being essentially similar in both) contains some genes not analogous to any on the X chromosome. So males and females differ significantly in the 'texture' of their DNA. Incidentally, the DNA of chimpanzees is closer to that of humans than it is to that of gorillas. This is because chimpanzees and humans are separated by a shorter period of evolutionary time than chimpanzees and gorillas. Thus chimpanzees are undoubtedly our closest relative.

A troop of chimpanzees is dominated by the alpha male. It couldn't be more androcentric. So one might argue that the reason for androcentrism is in our genes. But that would be wrong. For a human is as closely related to a bonobo or pygmy chimpanzee (*Pan paniscus*) as it is to the common chimpanzee (*Pan troglodytes*). And bonobos are entirely matriarchal. It is

3

the alpha female who rules the roost. When a male approaches with a desire for sex, a female bonobo will not meekly submit if she doesn't feel like it, but will fight him off. As he retreats wounded, he will probably turn to another male for sex. Homosexuality among bonobos — male and female — is rife. Female leadership among animals is not so uncommon. Hyenas, horses, macaques, vervet monkeys, spotted hyenas and elephants all live in female-dominant groups. But many factors concerning a particular troupe influence the outcome, not just the sex of the individual [8]. In short, analogies with animals do not help us to decide whether androcentrism is innate or acquired.

Two other physical attributes that differ between men and women are the deeper voice and hirsute face. According to an ancient text, 'a low-pitched voice indicated manly courage, a high-pitched voice female cowardice' [9]. Not surprising that during the 1980s, British prime minister Margaret Thatcher was persuaded to lower her voice during speeches so as to sound less strident and more authoritative. The Egyptian Queen Hatshepsut (chapter 3) had herself shown on monuments in male attire with an impressive beard. Such tricks may help women to appear more manly, but neither a deep voice nor a hirsute face — any more than muscularity — explains men's perceived right to control the lives of women.

What about hormonal influences? The sex hormones, like testosterone and estrogens, affect not only physical features but also the brain. A major target is the hypothalamus, but another is the structure known as the hippocampus. This is the site for memory, spatial recognition and emotion. The greater empathy attributed to women, which is particularly important in regard to childbearing, is modulated by such hormones. So are moods like kindness and acquiescence. Perhaps these are as intrinsic in females, as belief in a natural superiority may be in males? An intriguing thought, but such feelings and emotions span both sexes. As with muscular power, there is overlap between the two in regard to any one emotion. And in each case the person-to-person variation is huge. For every Mother Teresa there is a Messalina, for every Genghis Khan a Dalai Lama. As the latter himself said in 2007, 'Although men and women have the same potentials for aggression and warm-heartedness, they differ in which of the two more easily manifests' [10]. Different combinations of hormones act on an essentially gender-neutral brain. Attempts to ascribe the cause of androcentrism to a particular set of hormones are unlikely to be fruitful.

I mentioned earlier that leadership in animals does not support the concept that the basis for androcentrism in humans is innate. On the other hand recent studies with mice have revealed interesting results in regard to emotion. I appreciate that mice resemble humans even less than do chimpanzees, but over the last 100 years they have paved the way for our understanding of human biochemistry and disease. This is because the function of organs like liver, heart or kidney is the same in mice and men. It is true of the brain as well. What differs is the relative size of the structures within the brain. Mice have a better sense of smell than humans, so the area of the brain devoted to sensing odours is enhanced. In contrast the frontal cortex, where thoughts are processed and decisions taken, is larger in humans. (This also represents the chief difference between the brain of a human and that of a chimpanzee. The frontal cortex of the former is much larger, in order to accommodate the three-fold increase in cortical neurons between human and chimpanzee.)

Many emotional responses in mammals originate with the sense of smell. This is perceived in the nose through a structure known as the vomeronasal organ (VNO). Such smells, known as pheromones, are transmitted from the VNO to the brain. A male mouse, for example, is sexually attracted to a female by her smell, transmitted through the VNO in his nose. Humans are less able to detect pheromones. We have a different type of VNO and with us, sexual attraction depends less on smell than it does in mice. I will not pursue this aspect further: this book is about female subjugation by men, not about sexual proclivities.

The study to which I wish to refer is one carried out by Harvard neuroscientist Catherine Dulac. She is the first to have isolated the VNO pheromone receptor (a protein) from mice. She next decided to eliminate a gene that is essential for a functioning VNO by a process known as 'gene knockout'. This produced mutant mice that could not transmit smells to the brain. Because pheromones from male mice induce aggressive behaviour in other male mice, Dulac wondered what would happen if a mutant male were confronted with a normal male. Far from attacking him, the mutant tried to mate with him! She then showed that a mutant male, when confronted with a newborn mouse (which a normal male would attack), will care for the pup, just like a female. 'This made us think that the mouse brain, whether it is male or female, has circuitry that triggers parental behavior, irrespective of whether the animal is male or female. ... I would say that until our work, there was this idea, at least for mammals, about rigid structural differences in the brain between males and females. What we found is that it is more complicated than that. ... Yes, there are early hormonal actions that make a male brain more prone to display male-typical behavior and a female more prone to display behavior that is female-typical. But that doesn't mean that those brains are so different that one cannot display the behavior of the other' [11].

That leaves Darwin's 'distinction in the intellectual powers of the two sexes'. Respected scientists like Ruben Gur at the University of Pennsylvania and Simon Baron-Cohen at the University of Cambridge have published widely on gender differences within the human brain. The former has used neuroimaging techniques to show 'sex differences, aging effects, and abnormalities in regional brain function associated with schizophrenia, affective disorders, stroke, epilepsy, movement disorders and dementia' [12]. The latter has developed a theory of autism based on gender. Baron-Cohen finds that women are better at empathising, men better at systemising [13]. The conclusions of both these authors regarding gender differences in the brain have been criticised by others, but that is not unusual in science.

Following on from Baron-Cohen, I note that the eminent Harvard biologist Edward Wilson considers that 'play differs as a genetic trait between boys and between girls, with boys prone to engage in imitation fighting, singly or in coalitions, as a way of expressing dominance' [14a]. Others consider that girls' preference for dolls and boys' for trains are innate. Medical TV presenter Michael Mosley recently went so far as to show young chimpanzees jumping from a tree and pouncing on children's playthings. You guessed it. Male and female chimpanzees each went for their gender-assumed toys. Such differences in behaviour may, however, be due to contrasting modes of upbringing, rather than reflecting an innate disparity between the sexes [14b].

The key question, of course, is whether any purported gender differences affect cognitive function. A recent review of sex hormone interactions with the brain is suggestive. 'Many neural and behavioral functions are affected, including mood, cognitive function, blood pressure regulation, motor coordination, pain, and opioid sensitivity. Subtle sex differences exist for many of these functions that are developmentally programmed by hormones and by not yet precisely defined genetic factors, including the mitochondrial genome. These sex differences and responses to sex hormones in brain regions, which influence functions not previously regarded as subject to such differences, indicate that we are entering a new era of our ability to understand and appreciate the diversity of gender-related behaviors and brain functions' [15]. The review shows that the prefrontal cortex is a potential target, but 'cognitive function' is not defined. I suspect that this has more to do with learning than with innate intellect.

An obvious problem in regard to intellectual ability is that — as with emotional states — the variation among individuals is enormous. If one takes 1,000, or 10,000, or 100,000 women and compares their IQ values with those of an equal number of men, what does one find? In each case the values will fall onto a bell-shaped curve. If the top of the bell — the mean value — is different in the two groups, can one conclude that one sex is intrinsically more intelligent than the other? In principle, perhaps; in actuality, no. This is because IQ is a reflection not only of 'nature' but also of 'nurture'. The contribution of each varies from one person to the next. If one assumes that approximately half the value is due to one's genes — male or female — it means that the other half is dependent on external influences such as upbringing, health, nutrition and so forth [16]. To establish two groups of volunteers that are identical in all such aspects of 'nurture' is virtually impossible.

Nevertheless, 'when it comes to intelligence ... it has been convincingly established that there are no differences between the average woman and man. Psychologist Roberto Colom at the Autonomous U of Madrid found negligible differences in "general intelligence" (a measure that takes into account intelligence, cognitive ability and mental ability) when he tested over ten thousand adults. ... His paper, published in *Intelligence* in 2000, confirms what earlier studies have repeatedly shown' [17].

Then there is maverick Anne Fausto-Sterling, Professor of Biology and Gender Studies at Brown University in Rhode Island. She proposes — somewhat provocatively — that individuals should be considered as an interacting system of five categories: male, female, and three other ones. Science journalist Angela Saini points out that 'only in this way, she argues, can we truly get to the heart of why women and men across the world appear to be so different from each other, when studies of mathematical ability, intelligence, motor skills and almost every other measure consistently tell us they're not' [18].

In her book *The Gendered Brain*, neuroscientist Gina Rippon concludes that 'decades of findings using increasingly sophisticated imaging techniques have not yielded anything like a consensus as to what might differentiate a 'male brain' from a 'female brain'. ... Meta-analyses by Janet Hyde in 2005 and Ethan Zell and colleagues in 2015 suggested that the overwhelming message from decades of research on millions of participants was that, actually women and men were more similar than they were different, with differences disappearing over time. ... So, as with brains, there is no such thing as a typically female behavioural profile or a typically male behavioural profile — each of us is a mosaic of different skills, aptitudes and abilities, and attempting to pigeon-hole us into two archaically labelled boxes will fail to capture the true essence of human variability' [19].

The debate continues and it is time to take a side. My view is that the potential for a high intellect is gender neutral. As Gina Rippon told me in December 2020 regarding measures of specific cognitive competence, 'None of these consistently find any sex differences and the data always show high levels of variance.' The structure of the brain is gender neutral. Its function in regard to feelings like empathy or aggression is modulated by hormonal influences but its function in regard to cognitive ability is not. The 'female brain' does not exist. By throwing my hat in with Gina

Rippon and the likes of science journalist Angela Saini, I may be labelled a feminist. I am proud to wear that badge (though I would prefer the simple word scientist). To conclude, men may be physically stronger, but their intellectual ability is no greater than that of women. The perceived superiority of males — androcentrism — is largely a cultural phenomenon. If so, when and why did it arise? That is what the rest of this book is about.

Notes

1. James Fitzjames Stephen: *Liberty, Equality, Fraternity* (2nd edition, ed by R J White; Cambridge: Cambridge University Press, 1997), p 194; quoted by Heffer (2014), p 620.

2. Ernest Barker: *Political Thought in England: 1848 to 1914* (London: Thornton Butterworth, 1915), p 150.

3. Both quotes taken from Roger Lewis' review of *The Case of the Married Woman* by Antonia Fraser in *The Sunday Telegraph* of 2 May 2021; the first quote appears on p 164, the second on p xvi of Antonia Fraser: *The Case of the Married Woman* (London: Weidenfeld and Nicolson, 2021).

4. quoted by Fara (2018), p 34.

5. Donaldson (1907), p 2.

6. Birgitta Glenmark *et al*: Difference in skeletal muscle function in male vs females: role of estrogen receptor-β. *American Journal of Physiology* **287**: E1125–E1131 (2004).

7. Pasternak (2003), Fig 1.1 on p 6.

8. Denise D Cummins: Dominance, Status and Social Hierarchies, in *The Handbook of Evolutionary Psychology*, pp 676–697 (2015).

9. Beard (2017), p 19.

10. StudyBuddhism.com; retrieved 2016-03-06.

11. Catherine Dulac Finds Brain Circuitry Behind Sex Specific Behaviors, *Quanta Magazine* (Dec 14, 2020).

12. From the Neurodevelopment and Psychosis Section of the University of Pennsylvania website.

13. David M Greenberg *et al*: Testing the Empathizing-Systemizing theory of sex differences and the Extreme Male Brain theory of autism in half a million people. *Proceedings of the National Academy of Sciences, USA* **115**: 12152–12157 (2018).

14a. Wilson (2017), p 115.

14b. Gina Rippon: Are girls really brainier than boys? *The Daily Telegraph (UK)* (13 August 2021).

15. Bruce S McEwen and Teresa A Milner: Understanding the broad influence of sex hormones and sex differences in the brain. *Journal of Neuroscience Research* **95**: 24–39 (2017).

16. Knopik *et al* (2017).

17. Saini (2017), p 85.

18. *ibid*, p 93.

19. Rippon (2019), p 335 *et seq.*

Chapter 2

Stirrings: The Neolithic Age

All across the world, from the Americas to Africa, from Europe to Australia, small bands of people are living by hunting and gathering. Their presence makes little impact on Earth: there are probably less than a million of them worldwide. Animals, not humans, dominate the globe. I am speculating about life around 20,000 years ago, towards the end of the Palaeolithic Age. Fully evolved modern humans (*H sapiens*), able to communicate with each other verbally, had displaced *H neanderthalensis* throughout Eurasia some 20,000 years earlier.

Let me backtrack a moment. The earliest *Homo* species, probably *H habilis*, evolved along the Great Rift Valley of eastern Africa 2–3 million years ago. Its ancestor, a species of *Australopithecus* (African ape), had been the first primate to walk on two feet. Various offspring of *H habilis* (such as *H erectus*, *H heidelbergensis*, *H neanderthalensis*) then emerged in Africa. None of these is the direct ancestor of *H sapiens*, which appeared around 300,000 years ago, possibly in northwest Africa but more likely in the Horn of Africa. The first to disperse out of the continent had been *H erectus*, who reached eastern China by about 1.8 million years ago before becoming extinct. They were followed by *H heidelbergensis*, named after the finding of a skull near Heidelberg in Germany, and *H neanderthalensis* or Neanderthal Man, in recognition of a skeleton discovered in the Neander valley to the east of Düsseldorf, also in Germany. These early humans — together with hippos and lions — had reached Europe as far west as Britain. This was still connected to the mainland by a land bridge, despite the fact that the last glacial age (approximately 2.5 million years to 11,700 years ago) had experienced a period of warming around 400,000 years ago. The climate continued to warm and by 125,000 years ago the land bridge had disappeared. By about 25,000 years ago Arctic conditions returned and Britain was once more connected to continental Europe [1]. The presence of Neanderthals during the warm period can be traced to sites from Swanscombe in southern England to the Balkans, from Uzbekistan to the Levant. They became extinct around 40,000 years ago.

We are the only living species of our genus, *Homo*. Butterflies, in contrast, number 18,500 separate species. Several waves of *H sapiens* left Africa. If the cranial remains found in a Greek cave, which were recently analysed and dated by novel techniques [2], are confirmed, the earliest *H sapiens* will have arrived in Europe shortly after their appearance in Africa. Although *neanderthalensis* and *sapiens* have long been considered to be separate species (and therefore unable to produce fertile offspring between them), recent analyses have revealed traces of *neanderthalensis* DNA in that of our own [3]. Some hanky-panky seems to have occurred before *neanderthalensis* became extinct.

Back to the Neolithic Age. The most recent glacial period would soon come to an end, but as yet the sea level was still 120 metres lower than subsequently. Perhaps because available food was running out, or on account of *H sapiens'* innate curiosity [4], intrepid groups in northern Siberia had wandered eastward across the Bering land bridge into present-day Alaska. From there, some then roamed all the way into South America [5a]. And from Southeast Asia, then a large land mass (Sunda), humans had managed to cross 90 km or so of open water into Papua New Guinea-Australia-Tasmania (Sahul) by 50,000 years ago.

The largest animals — woolly mammoth in the northern regions, zebra in Africa — demand masculine muscles to bring them down with flint-edged wooden spears, but all in all hunting was probably a joint effort between males and females. In fact there is recent evidence that women hunted large animals [5b]. Childbearing alone was the sole domain of women. Most other tasks were shared, with children joining in. Deer, ducks and geese, eggs from the nests of birds and honey from those of wasps, fruit and nuts, nettles and dandelions, contributed to the diet. To ensure a supply of drinking water these nomadic people lived mainly near lakes and rivers. Here, as well as at the seashore, fish and shellfish were prized sources of food: a large catfish or salmon, caught with a barbed spear made of wood, could feed a large group for several weeks.

The control of fire by early humans (not yet *H sapiens*) at least a million years ago led directly to the cooking [6] of animal carcasses to make them easier to chew. As a result the intake of protein was greatly enhanced, which probably influenced the growth of the human brain in ancestral *Homo* species. So by 20,000 years ago the use of fire was well established. This will have helped to keep the inhabitants of the northern regions warmer than they would otherwise be in the shelter of caves. In addition they wrapped the skins of animals around them. Elsewhere, little clothing covered their bodies. It has recently been suggested that some may have suffered from a type of coronavirus [7].

When not scavenging for food, some of the people found time to express themselves through art. Cave and wall paintings executed with charcoal and ochre, dating back even earlier than the Mesolithic, have been found in Europe, India, Australia, South Africa and North America. I myself have admired ancient wall art when visiting the bristle cone pine forest in the White Mountains of eastern California. In fact the art of 20,000 years ago is already a more sophisticated version, in terms of accurate depictions of human figures and animals, than that of 40,000 years ago. And a flute made of the bone of a vulture that dates back to the latter figure has recently been found in Germany's Swabian Alps.

From this description regarding the lifestyle of the inhabitants of the globe 20,000 years ago, it is clear that they were already quite advanced. Yet it is probable that sexual intercourse was still rather random, with little evidence of monogamy and the two-adult family. This, together with an apparent equality between the two sexes, shows that androcentrism had not yet reared its ugly head. It would not do so for at least another ten millennia, during the Neolithic Age. I should point out that in this regard I differ from the founders of sociology in the 19th century who appear to have assumed patriarchy — androcentrism — to be a fundamental characteristic of the human species. One of their number was the polymath and champion of Darwin's theory of natural selection, Herbert Spencer. He supported moves for the enfranchisement of women, though he was diffident about the timing. If his remark that 'perhaps in no way is the moral progress of mankind more clearly shown, than by contrasting the position of women among savages with their position among the most advanced of the civilized' [8] is taken as sarcasm, then he was one of the first to query the prevalent view that androcentrism is innate. I return to this topic in the next chapter.

At the beginning of the Holocene [9], something extraordinary happened in different parts of the world. (From now on I will not use 'years ago' unless appropriate, and will employ the more precise 'BCE' — 'Before the Common Era'; but note that most of the dates are still approximate, to +/– a few hundred years). In around 10000 BCE in Anatolia it occurred to some — as likely as not women — to try to reproduce the seeds they had been gathering to feed their children by planting them: the cultivation of wheat and barley was born. Around 8000 BCE in middle China, rice was grown. In central America, maize, beans and squash were being developed. Such domestication of crops — followed in some cases by animal husbandry, in others preceded by it — arose independently in different regions of the world. The first to suggest this, in 1924, was the Russian scientist Nikolai Vavilov [10]. Vavilov travelled throughout the world, collecting and analysing native plants and came to the conclusion that there were some eight independent areas in which agriculture was born. Since then, Papua New Guinea has been identified as another (Figure 2.1).

Vavilov was an exceptionally gifted scientist. He thought that by careful breeding and selection of wild varieties of wheat and other cereals that he found growing in extremely cold climates, he could produce a more nutritious variety that grew well in the harsh climate of central Russia. This could reverse the famine that had resulted from Stalin's disastrous collectivisation programme. Stalin was intrigued and gave Vavilov three years to produce the necessary seeds. Vavilov pointed out that it would take ten to twelve years. That was because he knew that direct adaptation to a new environment, as proposed by the 18th-century French scientist Jean-Baptiste Lamarck, does not occur. Let me give you an example. If you decide to move to live at a very high altitude like the Andes where oxygen

Figure 2.1   Origins of agriculture. Areas 1–8 are based on researches by Nikolai Vavilov during the 1930s [Vavilov (2009)]. Since then they have been redefined and reduced to just five major areas: see the text. Area 9 in Papua New Guinea, said to have been developed between 10,000 and 7,000 years ago, was more recently added by Gideon Ladizinsky [Ladizinsky (1998)]. Adapted from Wikipedia; licensed under CC BY-SA 4.0.

levels are low, the bone marrow will respond by producing more red blood cells to offset the lack of oxygen. But the genes in the germ cells will be unaffected, and your progeny will be born in the same state as you were in originally. The native dwellers at high altitudes tolerate low oxygen levels because over many generations the ability to produce higher amounts of red blood cells have gradually been selected for. This is the essence of the evolutionary theory proposed by Charles Darwin and Alfred Wallace in the mid-19th century, which had been accepted by all serious scientists by the 1930s. But not by maverick geneticist Trofim Lysenko.

In order to ingratiate himself with Stalin, Lysenko assured him that he could breed the necessary seeds within three years. Stalin backed Lysenko, arrested Vavilov as a 'reactionary' and sent him to the Gulag where he died of starvation in 1943. Lysenko received the highest honours and was appointed to top positions. But his agricultural programme was a disaster. Thirty million starved to death (half of these in China where Mao Zedong followed Lysenko's agenda). When I was invited by the Soviet Academy of Sciences to give some talks in the late 1980s, my hosts were embarrassed by the fact that genetics research in the Soviet Union had been stalled for 50 years in consequence of the ludicrous ideas imposed by Lysenko (he did not die until 1976). 'Well, at least you put the first man into space,' I countered. They were not impressed.

It is time to return to the Neolithic. The centres of origin since Vavilov's time have been redefined and reduced to six: the southeast of North America (4000–3000 BCE) where swamp elder, squash and sunflower, followed much later by knot grass, barley and millet, were domesticated; Central America (9000–4000 BCE): peppers and avocados, then maize, squash and pumpkin, then beans; western South America (6000 BCE): lima beans, groundnuts and potatoes (as well as guinea pigs, llamas and alpacas); Anatolia (10,000–9000 BCE): barley, spelt and emmer wheat, lentils, peas and vetch (as well as sheep and goats, followed by pigs from wild boars and cattle from aurochs); China (8500 BCE): soya in the north, rice in the south; and Papua New Guinea (10000 BCE; remember *H sapiens* had reached this region 40,000 years earlier): taro (as well as pigs) [11].

What were the reasons for this development, sometimes referred to as the 'Neolithic Revolution'? An explanation based on climate change — the Oasis Theory — was proposed some time ago by the Australian archaeologist Vere Gordon Childe [12]. He suggested that increased periods of drought and desiccation in the near East around 9700 BCE caused people to congregate at oases and river valleys. Over a relatively short period of time — a few hundred years — such human proximity increased the population to the point where it was no longer able to survive by foraging alone. This led them to explore new ways for obtaining food. Childe's hypothesis may be correct as far as farming in Mesopotamia is concerned, but the reason for independent beginnings of agriculture in places as far apart, and as ecologically distinct, as middle China, central America or the Sahel region of Africa where cattle were being reared by 5000 BCE (approximately area 5 of Figure 2.1), is not at all clear.

The time-consuming domestication of wild crops, by sowing their seeds and selecting for the best plants over many generations, may indeed, as mentioned, have been carried out by women, while the domestication of animals was done by men. Of course, we cannot be sure. From analysis of early human remains we have been able to deduce what kinds of food they ate and from what diseases and accidents they suffered. But who precisely did what, we do not know. Many tasks were probably shared. For no good reason I am prepared to accept the views of today's feminists that it was women who first cultivated crops. It is then to them that we owe the appearance of the plants mentioned above. And to the menfolk the domestication of pigs from wild boars and cattle from aurochs. The practice of farming required new tools. A primitive scythe for harvesting, a flat stone on which to grind grain with a smaller one, pens in which to contain domesticated animals — all made of stone and wood. I will not attempt to assign ownership of these inventions to either sex. Women proved capable of carrying out male jobs during the two world wars of the 20th century, and today we find them serving alongside men in the armed forces and police, as well as making scientific discoveries previously considered the preserve of men. I fancy that during Neolithic times women and men shared tasks far more than we realise.

One of the earliest records of farming points to Anatolia, to the north of the Arabian desert, as the birthplace of agriculture. However, the recent identification of Papua New Guinea as another original centre [13] has challenged this somewhat. The Anatolian region has been dubbed the 'Fertile Crescent' (Figure 2.2). The centre of the Crescent is near Göbekli Tepe in present-day southern Turkey. This site has been excavated by German archaeologist Klaus Schmidt and dated to 10000–8000 BCE. It contains several stone circles — probably the oldest in the world — that presumably served some kind of ritual function before any town buildings were constructed [14a]. A recent report [14b] suggests that its people were sustained by a carbohydrate-rich diet of wild grains that were pounded into a paste and consumed in a manner akin to porridge. From such grains they also made beer. This contrasts with the view that prior to the agricultural revolution, Neolithic humans lived on a 'low carb' diet. For at Göbekli Tepe there are no signs of any farming practices. The domestication of cereal and other crops — as well as animal husbandry — was still unknown.

One arm of the Crescent extends south westwards into present-day Syria and beyond to Jordan and Israel; the other arm south eastwards into present-day Iraq towards the Persian Gulf. Within the Crescent, some 20 sites where agriculture was being practised by 10000–9500 BCE have been identified. From here, agriculture — farming and the domestication of animals — spread westwards into Europe, northwards and eastwards into Asia, and southwards into Africa. The novel practices reached Spain, the Caspian and north Africa by 7000 BCE, Britain, India and Africa's rainforests by 5000 BCE, and Scandinavia and southern Africa by 2000 BCE [15]. Secondary migrations occurred for climatic reasons. As the Sahara west of the Nile began to turn from grassland to desert around 5000 BCE, primitive farmers moved to the banks of the great river to begin cultivating the fertile land along its banks. Thus was the grandeur of Pharaonic Egypt born. Another river that gave rise to an ancient civilisation is the Indus, where the Harappa people were growing wheat and barley by 3000 BCE. And the eastern arm of the Crescent itself spawned the Sumerian empire and its followers (chapter 3).

Figure 2.2   The Fertile Crescent. This corresponds to area 4 of Figure 2.1. Adapted from Wikipedia; licensed under CC BY-SA 4.0.

Moving from a nomadic to a more settled life with an abundant supply of food led to an increase in the population: from 10 million worldwide to 50 million between 8000 and 3000 BCE. It doubled to 100 million over the next millennium, largely due to the hydraulic techniques being developed along the banks of the Nile, the Euphrates and Tigris, and the Indus. Between 1000 BCE and 1000 CE such methodology enabled rice to be cultivated in China, India and Southeast Asia, as well as maize, beans, potatoes and other products by the pre-Inca Olmec, Maya and Aztec cultures of the Americas. All this resulted in an increased rate of population growth to 250 million [16]. Small communities developed into villages, though as Heather Pringle has pointed out, 'in many regions, settlements came thousands of years after crops, while in others, villages appear long before intensive agriculture, implying a long, slow transition to the agrarian way of life' [17].

Grazing cattle, sheep and goats provides a nutritious source of food: the carbohydrate lactose in milk. Lactose is a disaccharide made up of a glucose and a galactose unit joined together. To absorb it requires the presence of lactase (an enzyme or protein catalyst), produced in the lining of the small intestine, which splits lactose into its constituent molecules, glucose ('blood sugar') and galactose, both of which are easily absorbed. All mammals produce lactase during lactation. Thereafter the enzyme disappears, and mammals like lions and tigers turn to eating meat as a major source of energy. Unabsorbed lactose is not merely lost energy, but is actually detrimental, causing abdominal pain, diarrhoea and other complications. Lactase deficiency in some humans today is a recognised genetic disorder. The arrival of agriculture meant that the gene for lactase was of selective advantage, and spread rapidly among dairy-farming people — perhaps over no more than a few thousand years. Other genetic changes evolve much more slowly: it took two million years for the brains of our ancestors to double in size. The ability to produce lactase in adulthood did not occur to the same extent in all farming people. Today lactose tolerance is higher in northern Europeans (up to 96%) than in those living in eastern and southern Europe (down to as little as 15%). It is clear that other genetic factors are involved [18].

Another disaccharide of nutritive value is sucrose ('table sugar'). It is made of glucose linked to fructose. They are released by an enzyme, sucrase, in the small intestine, just like lactase. In contrast, sucrase is present throughout life in most animals. The main source of sucrose during Neolithic times in Europe would have been from honey and fruits.

Sugarcane was domesticated in Papua New Guinea around 6000 BCE, and independently in Southern China from 5500 BCE. From there it reached India, whose inhabitants discovered how to extract the sugar and then to crystallise it. Cultivation of sugarcane was brought to the Mediterranean by Arab traders after 700 CE: the Romans knew sugar only as a medicine, not as food. It was Christopher Columbus who, on his second voyage, planted the first seedlings of sugarcane in the New World [19]. The consequences proved disastrous for the under-privileged inhabitants of West Africa for the next 300 years.

The domestication of animals led to the first glimmerings of gender inequality among the Kurgan tribes. Kurgan is a Russian word that refers to a mound, under which people were buried, rather like the tumuli of Anglo-Saxon England (it is also the name of a Russian town in the south of the Urals). The Kurgan, who inhabited the Pontic-Caspian steppes between and to the north of the Black and Caspian Seas, from the mouth of the Dniester in the west to that of the Ural River to the east (see Figure 3.1 in the following chapter), were early breeders of cattle. Because cattle and sheep are easier to steal than plants, they became a more valuable resource. This led to the appearance of chiefs, for 'domestic animals can only be raised by people who are committed morally and ethically to watching their families go hungry rather than letting them eat the breeding stock. Seed grain and breeding stock must be saved, not eaten, or there will be no crop and no calves next year. ... It is not surprising that it was resisted, or that when it did begin it was surrounded by new rituals and a new kind of leadership ...' [20]. Kurgan mythology was 'at its core, the world view of male-centered, cattle-raising people.' [21]. The same was true elsewhere. In Africa, for example, 'cattle-raising seems to have led to the loss of matrilineal social organizations and the spread of male-patrilineal kinship systems' [22]. The self-assured superiority of the cattle-owning Tutsi over the peasant Hutu in Rwanda was one of the factors that led to the genocide of 1994 [23].

The herding of cattle in the Pontic-Caspian steppes, then, led to social inequality: 'Cattle-herding was not just a new way to get food; it also supported a new division of society between high-status and ordinary people, a social hierarchy that had not existed when daily sustenance was based on fishing and hunting' [24]. The villages that grew out of the practice of agriculture also resulted in the emergence of hierarchies [25] to deal with administrative matters as the population density increased. Do such hierarchies, based on affluence and influence, lead inevitably to androcentrism, the most extreme form of hierarchies? Or is it the other way round? Or is there no connection between the two?

Historians seem reluctant to answer this question. One who appears to attempt it is Gerda Lerner whose *The Creation of Patriarchy* was referred to earlier. In reviewing this book, author Virginia Hunter writes that 'in time, out of the labour of women as reproducers, private property was created' and continues, quoting Lerner, 'in the course of the agricultural revolution the exploitation of human labor and the sexual exploitation of women became inextricably linked' [26]. Whether one agrees with that or not, it is 'culture' as well as 'agri' which epitomises every civilisation that emerged (chapters 3 and 4). And in each civilisation the seeds of androcentrism began to flourish.

But human developments like agriculture and the appearance of towns happened at different times in different places. Gerda Lerner's remark about the emergence of patriarchy was in reference to Mesopotamia between the 4th and 2nd millennium BCE. In Europe towns were still in their infancy at this time. Rural communities continued to live in gender-neutral societies. For example, in one settled group living in the Le Vigneau region of northwest France between 4720 and 4350 BCE, access to food was equal for males and females: isotopic analysis of their buried remains showed 'no strong trace of a patrilocal structure'. The graves included weapons for hunting, which indicates that they were not yet herders of domesticated animals [27].

As mentioned earlier, there are instances where the emergence of villages preceded that of agriculture. Over a century ago, a 36-year-old British archaeologist, Dorothy Garrod (who would become the first female holder of a professorship at Cambridge), was excavating a cave on the west bank of the Jordan, near Jericho. What she found here and in neighbouring sites were stone implements dating back to the Mesolithic period,

12500–9500 BCE. These and other factors caused Garrod to suggest that a sedentary community — probably the oldest in the world — lived here. They appear to have made bread and beer from wild barley, which they domesticated only some time later. Garrod called this culture Natufian, after the name of the valley in which some of these people lived [28].

The other example of village life preceding agriculture is along the coast of northwest America, stretching from southern Alaska down to Washington State. These were the original inhabitants of the Americas who had migrated eastwards out of northeast Siberia between 20,000–10,000 years ago. Unlike their compatriots who continued their trek all the way south to Tierra del Fuego, some hundred different tribes decided to settle along the forested shores and the islands close by. They were sedentary, often matriarchal, societies living largely off the sea — including whale meat — where they even developed fish farms. Yet no land-based agriculture was developed. On the other hand they began to work copper into ceremonial shields 3,000 years ago, and their skill at wood carving on long totem poles has continued until the present. They were clever enough to begin trading seal fur with the English- and Spanish-speaking people who arrived from the mainland, and with the Russians who sailed in from the west, in the late 18th century. But their fate was sealed. The smallpox brought in (deliberately) by the Europeans, as elsewhere, decimated their numbers. Today the survivors proudly continue their handicrafts but they, and their art, are no more than museum pieces [29].

Can some of the artifacts found at ancient sites tell us anything about the gender relations of their creators? Lithuanian-born Marija Gimbutas, Professor of European Archaeology and Indo-European Studies at the University of California Los Angeles [30], certainly thought so. In an area which she defines as 'Old Europe' (Figure 2.3), she has unearthed hundreds of figurines and decorated vases made of fired clay, as well as ornaments of gold and copper, and other objects made of stone and bone. Many of the wares depict a corpulent 'Fertility' or 'Mother' Goddess, often holding her arms over large breasts. These artifacts have been dated to around 6500–3500 BCE and found associated with settlements and villages

Figure 2.3   Old Europe *c* 7000–3500 BCE. Adapted from Gimbutas (1982), p 16.

(but not yet towns). As the inhabitants of this region began the practice of agriculture, a Pregnant Vegetation Goddess, associated with the fecundity of nature as well as that of humans, appeared. Over 5,000 years later, we still refer to 'Mother Nature'. Other goddesses are part snake, bird, egg and fish. Many are deliberately symbolic and seem to have been associated with specific rituals. It is from this wealth of female artifacts that Gimbutas assumes their creators to have lived in an essentially peaceful, matriarchal society. So sophisticated are some of the objects that 'if one defines civilization as the ability of a given people to adjust to its environment and to develop adequate arts, technology, script, and social relationships it is evident that Old Europe achieved a marked degree of success' [31].

The Neolithic, and later Chalcolithic (copper-producing) peoples of Old Europe, are not the direct ancestors of today's Europeans. The motifs of some of the artifacts can be recognised on the Minoan frescoes of the 2nd millennium BCE found at Knossos in Crete, and aspects of the ritual beliefs of these Old Europeans are found in Greek mythology a millennium later, but that should not imply a continuity of generations. For 'the earliest European civilization was savagely destroyed by the patriarchal element' of the Proto-Indo-Europeans 'and it never recovered, but its legacy lingered in the substratum which nourished further European cultural developments' [32]. Who were these interlopers?

In fact I have already mentioned them: the Kurgan people of the Russian steppe. This area, which stretched eastward from the mouth of the Dniester across Ukraine and southern Russia as far as the Ural Mountains, is also referred to as the North Pontic region. Its inhabitants were a hardy people who had acquired the domestication of animals from farmers in Old Europe. Some of these herders, or pastoralists, had migrated north eastward from Greece and the Danube basin of Old Europe into the North Pontic region around 5200 BCE. Here they settled for several millennia. Their neighbours to the north and east continued to hunt and gather. The Kurgan people are also known as Proto-Indo-European speakers. Whereas agriculture had diffused from Anatolia to the southwest and southeast without the movement of people, rather like a row of dominos falling each upon its neighbour, and the Black Death was spread from Asia to Europe by rats not people, the dissemination of Indo-European languages resulted from the migration of Kurgan tribes westwards as far as Ireland, eastwards to India, and southwards into Persia. They carried with them the roots of the Indo-European languages which developed into a unique tongue wherever they settled. They were not invaders like the descendants of Genghis Khan, who with their Mongolian horsemen devastated all before them as they rode westward as far as Central Europe in the 13th century. The Kurgans traded with the original inhabitants and interbred with them. They brought new technologies like the wheel. But they also brought the seeds of androcentrism that would dominate Eurasia for the next 5,000 years. I will return to this aspect in the following chapter.

Notes

1. Tate Greenhalgh and Lisa Hendry: *The Making of an Island*, from https://www.nhm.ac.uk/discover/the-making-of-an-island.html.
2. Katerina Harvati *et al*: Apidima Cave fossils provide earliest evidence of Homo sapiens in Eurasia. *Nature* **571**: 500–504 (2019).
3. Sykes (2020).
4. Charles Pasternak: *Curiosity and Quest*, in Pasternak (2007), pp 114–132.
5a. The evidence for a human presence as far south in the Americas as Santa Elena in present-day Brazil by 20,000 years ago has recently been strengthened. Ruth Gruhn: Evidence grows for early peopling of the Americas. *Nature* **584**: 47–48 (2020).
5b. Maya Wei-Haas: Prehistoric female hunter discovery upends gender role assumptions. *National Geographic* (4 November 2020).
6. Richard Wrangham: *The Cooking Enigma*, in Pasternak (2007), pp 182–203; subsequently expanded in Wrangham (2009).
7. Epidemic of 25,000 years ago may be key to treatment: *Sunday Telegraph* (22 November 2020).
8. quoted by Evans-Pritchard (1965), p 37.
9. Holocene describes a period from a geological aspect, whereas Palaeolithic and Neolithic refer to periods of human development. The Holocene began 12,000 years ago and has lasted until the Anthropocene — the period during which human actions have begun to affect Earth's climate; the start date has yet to be agreed internationally.
10. Pringle (2009).
11. Mazoyer and Roudart (2003), p 72 *et seq*.
12. Childe (1928).
13. Ladizinsky (1998).
14a. Curry (2008).
14b. Andrew Curry: The ancient carb revolution. Well before people domesticated crops, they were grinding grains for beer and hearty dishes. *Nature* **594**: 488–491 (2021).
15. Mazoyer and Roudart (2003), p 72.
16. *ibid*, p 63.
17. Heather Pringle: The slow birth of agriculture. *Science* **282**: 1446 (1998).

18. Pascale Gerbault *et al*: Evolution of lactase persistence. *Philosophical Transactions of the Royal Society B: Biological Sciences* **366**: 863–877 (2011).

19. Parker (2011).

20. Anthony (2007), p 155.

21. *ibid*, p 135.

22. Clare Holden and Ruth Mace: Spread of cattle led to the loss of matriliny in Africa. *Philosophical Transactions of the Royal Society B: Biological Sciences* **270**: 2425–2433 (2003), quoted in Anthony (2007), p 138.

23. see, for example, Pasternak (2018), pp 213–229.

24. Anthony (2007), p 132.

25. T Douglas Price: *Social Inequality at the Origins of Agriculture*, in Price and Feinman (1995).

26. Virginia Hunter: The origins of patriarchy: gender and class in the ancient world. *Labour/Le Travail* **22**: 239–246 (1988).

27. Gwenaëlle Goude *et al*: A multidisciplinary approach to Neolithic life reconstruction. *Journal of Archaeological Method and Theory* **26**: 537–560 (2019).

28. Brian Boyd: *Twisting the Kaleidoscope: Dorothy Garrod and the Natufian Culture*, in Davies and Charles (1999), pp 209–223.

29. Jago Cooper: *Masters of the Pacific Coast: The Tribes of the American Northwest*, from https://theartsdesk.com/tv/masters-pacific-coast-tribes-american-northwest-bbc-four.

30. Ernestine S Elster: Marija Gimbutas, 1921–1994. *American Journal of Archaeology* **98**: 755–757 (1994).

31. Gimbutas (1982), p 17.

32. *ibid*, p 238.

Chapter 3

Arrival: The Bronze Age and Early Civilisations

Describing the evolution of the Earth's crust since its formation 4.5 billion years ago in terms of geological periods works well. Dividing the time since humans first appeared into the Stone Age (Palaeolithic, Mesolithic and Neolithic), Chalcolithic (copper), Bronze Age and Iron Age produces discrepancies, since humans began these activities at different times in different parts of the world. I have mentioned this in regard to agriculture in the previous chapter. It is equally true for the development of metal technologies. Copper was being smelted in the Balkans during the 5th millennium BCE. The resulting artefacts were typical of the enlightened Vinca culture that developed, but then declined, in this region. Bronze, an alloy of copper and tin, was being used in Mesopotamia, along the Indus valley and in Egypt (partly: copper was still the dominant metal) by 3000 BCE. The technology did not reach Western countries such as Britain until 1,000 years later. At about that time, the Shang in China independently began to employ objects made of bronze. In the Americas the first use of bronze was probably by the Moche culture in northern Peru between 200 BCE and 600 CE. In Africa bronze was being fashioned in Benin by the 13th century (well before the arrival of Europeans). How did the manufacture of objects made of copper or bronze come about? Many millennia after the agricultural revolution, makers of pottery realised that fashioning objects by hand was not the only way to achieve a particular shape. For they had discovered that if some coloured rocks — blue, green, red, gold — are heated in a furnace, they melt. In the case of red ores, it is the copper in them that melts when heated to around 1,100°C. The fluid can then be poured into stone or clay containers of any desired shape. On cooling back to a solid, the shape is retained. How this discovery was made is unclear. Perhaps those sitting around a campfire adjacent to metal-containing rocks noticed that as the rocks became very hot, they began to melt [1]. The first objects made were largely trinkets. By experimenting with other rocks, it was found that if those that had a sheen to them (now known to contain tin) were added to copper-containing ones and heated, the resultant solid was much stronger. Gradually copper, then bronze, replaced implements made of stone [2].

Marija Gimbutas has detailed the areas of copper and tin deposits (as well as gold and amber, which can be extracted without the need for smelting) throughout Europe [3]. Tin is far less abundant than copper, which is why the Kurgans of the Pontic-Caspian steppes, who brought metallurgy as well as androcentrism into 'old Europe', worked mainly with the latter metal. The use of iron, to make even stronger tools and weapons, arrived some two millennia later. The reason for this is that in order to extract the reddish-coloured iron ore, higher temperatures are required. Iron melts only at about 1,500°C, but if carbon in the form of charcoal is added the melting temperature is reduced to 1,150°C. Because hard woods such as those found in the sub-Saharan forests burn at higher temperatures than other woods, iron smelting is evident already at around 1000 BCE in Nigeria (whereas bronze was relatively unknown, except much later as mentioned above).

Farming had already resulted in more static communities than before. Metal working amplified this and led to the allocation of specific duties, out of which hierarchies developed. Certainly by around 2000 BCE, social inequalities — servants and masters — were evident within individual households living in areas such as the Lech Valley in southern Germany [4]. Moreover, 'in a Bronze Age village we often find one hut, that was obviously the smithy' [5], implying a superior quarter. The high status of smelters around 1000 BCE has also been revealed in the area of a mine in the Sinai desert, some twelve miles north of the Red Sea at a place called Slave Hill. Here archaeologists have found traces of upper-class food — dates from elsewhere and fish from the Mediterranean 100 miles away, as well luxury clothing from Egypt [6]. The strenuous task of metal working was presumably carried out by men, so the hierarchy of the rich versus the poor was male-gendered. In contrast there is evidence that in China during the Shang Dynasty, bronze smelting may have been a family business, with women contributing to this taxing work [7].

One can see the emergence of wealth through the objects found buried alongside the dead. The graves of male skeletons buried with valuable weapons and other items made of copper or bronze greatly outnumbered those of females. The main point, however, is that 'the richest are remarkable not only for their splendour but also for the amount of potential wealth encapsulated in them and thus lost to the society that produced them. It is hard to think of this process in terms other than those of aggrandisement of the few, the rise of the élite, and the start of social stratification. Once acquired, this habit was never lost ...' [8].

Towards the end of the Bronze Age, the benefits of salt for preserving food seem to have been realised. For the people of upper Austria began to mine this commodity at a site now recognised as the oldest in the world. This is in Hallstadt near Salzburg (hence the latter's name). The production of salt became so much in demand — its use to preserve meat had been recognised — that a whole community, largely farming but also metal working, grew up here during the 1st millennium BCE. Trade in raw materials and goods, such as bronze and other artifacts, established a new profession: the merchant. All these activities were probably carried out by men. Competition for resources between communities occasionally led to conflicts in which the stronger males held sway. But the main reason why many of the administrative roles in villages were occupied by men is probably the simple fact that women were too busy caring for their offspring. So a gradual acceptance of the superiority of men over women ensued.

Like farming six millennia earlier, the invention of metal working had moved down the eastern arm of the Fertile Crescent (Figure 2.2 of chapter 2) into Mesopotamia (present-day Iraq). In fact, raw copper had been found at Çayönü Tepesi in Anatolia long before the advent of smelting. The metal was fashioned into trinkets and implements by cold beating.

Agriculture and metal working are two transformational technologies that would eventually be rationalised into the sciences of breeding (genetics) in the 20th century, and of metallurgy (chemistry) in the 19th.

Mesopotamia

Since the agricultural revolution, people throughout Europe had been living in hamlets and villages. They would continue to do so throughout the Bronze Age. But in Mesopotamia (literally 'between rivers'), larger units were emerging. An expanding production of food along the fertile banks of the Euphrates and Tigris led to an increase in the population. The advantages of urban life included larger markets, sharing of natural resources and better opportunities for trade. Uruk, considered to be the oldest city in the world, had all of these. It was situated along the left bank of the Euphrates, around 300 km south of modern-day Baghdad. Extensive excavations by German archaeologists during 1912–1913 indicate that the city was probably founded during the 4th millennium BCE. It was spread over an area of some 5.5 km^2 (550 hectares) and by 3000 BCE contained around 40,000 inhabitants [9]. In modern terms Uruk would be considered no more than a small town. But in its time no settlement in Europe, Asia or Egypt could match it for size.

Uruk's inhabitants were protected by a 9-km-long wall around the entire conurbation. Beyond the wall was a canal encircling the city that provided access through a number of waterways. These criss-crossed the city to bring water alongside its palace and temples. A plan of the area, showing the positions of the major buildings, can be found in the art book published by the J Paul Getty Museum [10]. The cosmopolitan life attracted people from further away. They settled close to the city, which in its heyday was home to 80,000–90,000 persons within and outside the urban environment [11]. The entire area between the Euphrates and the Tigris is a vast floodplain, without forests or rocky outcrops. To the northeast are the Zagros mountains of Persia, to the northwest the Syrian highlands. In order to obtain timber for its temple roofs, and copper for weapons and tools, Uruk traded textiles with towns like Susa nestling south of the Zagros range, and those to the northwest. Uruk's introduction of cuneiform writing (see below) and other inventions radiated outwards — eastward to Susa and southward to Egypt — but little returned. Uruk was definitely a first.

Countless statues and images (in alabaster, gypsum, limestone and other materials) of an imposing figure called The Great Man of Uruk have been discovered and dated to 3300–3000 BCE. He is tall, wears a loincloth and covering on his head, and when depicted with other men always exceeds them in height. Sometimes he is shown with a dead lion at his feet, sometimes raising his arms above his head. He appears to be a ruler in the heavens as well as a powerful man on Earth: a Priest King. Statues of women have also been unearthed. A tall figure, who may be the Goddess-Priestess Inanna, is seen together with the Great Man of Uruk. These figures probably 'embody core social values and established ideas about governance and not necessarily historic characters or specific events' [12].

A little further downstream, on the right bank of the Euphrates, another city grew up 1,000 years later. This was Ur. Together with other settlements, the surrounding area became known as Sumer. The language spoken by its inhabitants is Sumerian. Its roots are unknown. It is neither an Indo-European language (see below) nor a Semitic one like Akkadian that infiltrated the area during the 3rd millennium BCE. What *is* known is that the language was recorded, in cuneiform characters on wet clay tablets which when dry survive much better than papyrus or paper. The topics dealt largely with administrative matters or poems like the *Epic of Gilgamesh*, legendary ruler of Uruk. Sumerian is thus one of the oldest written languages in the world. From this time onwards, historians have been able to use ancient scripts to confirm and amplify (or disprove) the assumptions previously made solely on the basis of archaeological finds.

Most of the inhabitants of Sumer lived by farming, though fish provided the bulk of their protein intake. Those who were not practising agriculture were digging channels to irrigate the land and to link villages together. 'It is often implied that Sumer derived much of its economic strength from irrigation, but in reality water provided an even more fundamental context for everyday life' [13]. The canals facilitated the movement not only of people but also of goods. But the Sumerians developed something much more important: the wheel and its offspring, wheeled carts. Clay tablets found in Uruk and radiocarbon dated to 3500–3370 BCE (subsequently revised to 3300–3100 BCE) include a pictograph of a wheeled wagon. This form of transport appeared in Europe as well. Pottery showing wheeled wagons and dated to around 3500 BCE has been found in the area of the Trichterbecker culture (modern Poland, eastern Germany and southern Denmark). Clay models of wheeled wagons dated to the same period also appear in graves of the Baden culture (Hungary). And the remains of actual wooden wagons buried under the kurgans of the Russian steppe have been dated to 3000–2000 BCE [14]. Whether wheeled wagons were developed independently in all these regions has not been resolved. Unlike farming they never appeared in pre-Columbian America at all (except — allegedly — on Mayan toys).

The world's first astronomers were probably Sumerian. A particularly clever one was observing the night sky as dawn was approaching some 5,000 years ago when he noticed a trail of light moving across the sky. He noted down the origin of the light in relation to the known constellations on a clay tablet. That tablet has been lost, but what appears to have been an accurate copy was made by an Assyrian scribe in the royal palace of Nineveh around 700 BCE. That clay tablet was discovered in the middle of the 19th century by archaeologist Austen Henry Layard during his excavation of Nineveh. Layard realised that the tablet with its cuneiform inscriptions was an important item and presented it to the British Museum. Now two scientists, at least as clever as the Sumerian astronomer, have been able to link the Sumerian astronomer's observation to the impact of a kilometre-sized asteroid in the Austrian alpine village of Köfels that occurred in the morning of 29 June 3123 BCE, an hour before sunrise [15].

When not observing trails of light moving across the sky, Sumerians were weaving cloth (a task carried out mainly by women), smelting metal from imported ores, working as scribes, or employed in building the temples and royal residence that were emerging. For as already mentioned, priesthood and kingship, which sometimes merged as they did in Pharaonic Egypt, had arrived. Thus Gilgamesh, legendary king of Uruk (there is no evidence that he actually existed), became one of Sumer's several gods. The Sumerians had a goddess as well. Inanna represented not just love and beauty, but also prostitution, war and justice. She appears on a third millennium seal as a slimmer, more attractive version of the fertile goddesses of 'old Europe' described by Marija Gimbutas.

While there are no records of Uruk kings, the names of more than twenty in neighbouring Ur during the 3rd millennium BCE are known [16]. 'Kings were men. The only female king in the Sumerian Kinglist, Ku-Baba of Kish, is characterised as a brothel keeper ... obviously a mockery that not only belittled the power-hungry "kings of Kish", but also bespeaks the attitude towards women in the male-dominated early Mesopotamian establishment' [17]. Note also that 'royal inscriptions and hymns describe kings' relations with goddesses, yet never mention queens' [18].

On the other hand, 'there are grounds to doubt that Sumerian social structure was strictly patriarchal, because accession through the female line was possible, and women occupied high positions in states, economy, and cult, could be head of a family, and had substantial legal rights' [19]. As far as family life is concerned, an edict written in 2600 BCE states that 'the wife should not be weak; marriage is positive because a married man is well cared for; family is supportive, an older brother is like a father, an older sister like a mother but a son should also be supportive of his mother and older sister; mother's words are like those of a god to be respected by the son ...' [20].

Towards the end of the 3rd millennium BCE there grew up another powerful city known as Akkad. It was situated downstream from Ur, near the mouth of the Euphrates. Its legendary King Sargon is said to have conquered most of Sumer to establish the Akkadian empire. I mention him only because he is reputed to be the father of one Enheduanna, a High Priestess and the world's first recorded poet [21]. It has been suggested that Enheduanna served the goddess Inanna, but also that the historical Enheduanna and the mythical Inanna are actually the same person. The author Clare Enders tells me that 'I have read a great deal of material that indicates that Enheduanna ... "formed" Inanna out of prior myths/deity of matriarchal origins in order to provide herself with a worthy occupation'.

One of the major consequences of Bronze Age urbanisation in Mesopotamia that was absent in Europe, then, was the concept of kingship — a ruler living in a privileged environment with power over all. This introduced a new situation. The holders of rank were almost universally male. But women related to such men as mother, wife or widow, could act independently in ways denied to those lower down the social scale. This state of affairs is particularly evident during the Middle Ages (chapter 5). It continued for another 500 years after that, with wealth gradually replacing noble status as a qualification. At the other end of the scale, larger and more hierarchical communities led to slavery. In Mesopotamia, it may be noted, female slaves were more numerous than male ones.

It was during the Bronze Age then that cities — sometimes more accurately described as city states — grew up alongside the two great rivers: Uruk, Ur, Akkad and Babylon (whose streets, now several metres beneath the surface, I have been privileged to tread) beside the Euphrates in the south, Nineveh and Nimrud by the Tigris in the north. Through internecine fighting (by the 17th century BCE the Babylonian empire occupied much of southern Mesopotamia) and invasion by Kassites from the Zagros mountains, Hittites from Carchemish in the Syrian hills to the north, Persians, Seleucids (remnants of Alexander's army spread throughout Eurasia), Parthians from the east, Romans from the west and Muslim Arabs from the south, few remnants survived. As anthropologist Robert McCormick Adams noted some time ago, 'Much of the central floodplain of the ancient Euphrates now lies beyond the frontiers of cultivation, a region of empty desolation. Tangled dunes, long disused canal levees, and the rubble-strewn mounds of former settlement contribute only low, featureless relief. Vegetation is sparse, and in many areas it is wholly absent. Rough, wind-eroded land surfaces and periodically flooded depressions form an irregular patchwork in all directions, discouraging any but the most committed traveller. To suggest the immediate impact of human life there is only a rare tent ... Yet at one time here lay the core, the heartland, the oldest urban, literate civilization in the world' [22].

Europe

The people of the Pontic-Caspian steppes (Figure 3.1), whose influence encompasses the end of the Neolithic and the beginning of the Bronze Age, did more than introduce the horse and androcentrism into 'old' Europe. They brought the very languages we speak — from Gaelic in Ireland to Urdu and Hindi in Asia (Figure 3.2). Six of the main branches, namely Baltic, Slavic, Germanic, Celtic, Italic, and Hellenic, include all the languages spoken in Europe today. The only exceptions are Finnish, Hungarian (Magyar), Estonian, Sámi (spoken in the most northern region of Finland and neighbouring Sweden, Norway and Russia), Basque (spoken in parts of France and Spain) and Maltese. The first four of these languages are known as Uralic and were most likely spoken by people from the region of the Ural mountains who preceded the arrival of the Kurgan tribes from the Pontic-Caspian steppes into western Europe. The origin of Basque is unknown, but it too is likely to have been spoken before the advent of the Kurgans. Maltese is of Arabic and therefore Semitic origin. The remaining branches, namely Armenian, Anatolian and Indo-Iranian, are spoken across southwestern Asia as far as the Brahmaputra River. The total number of Indo-European speakers today accounts for roughly half the population of the world.

The Proto-Indo-European language (PIE) is unknown, since it was never written down and the present residents of the Pontic-Caspian region do not speak it. The language is extinct. It is assumed to be the mother of all Indo-European languages, by working backwards from the languages known to have been spoken at different times. The reason for grouping languages together is based on sound systems, comparative grammar and syntax. The first of these that may be illustrated is the word for 100. The Italic branch (Figure 3.2) produced *centum* in Latin (pronounced *kentum* but leading to *cent*, *cento* and *cien* in French, Italian and Spanish respectively); the Germanic branch produced *hunt* in Old High German and *hund*

Figure 3.1   The Proto-Indo-European Homeland around 3,500–3,000 BCE. Adapted from
Anthony (2007), p 84.

in Old English (leading to *hundert* in German and *hundred* in English); the
Baltic branch produced *shimtas* in Lithuanian. From the way these were
pronounced, polymath David Anthony deduces that the original word in
PIE was something like *k'mtom* [23].

Sanskrit is a product of the Indo-Iranian branch. Historian and TV
documentary presenter Neil Oliver has pointed out that 'the Sanskrit for
"war" means, literally, "the hunger for more cows". "Chattel", which is
close to "cattle", is the earliest word for any kind of personal property' [24],

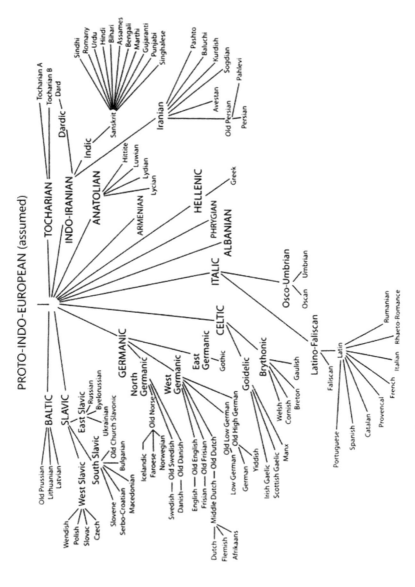

Figure 3.2   Indo-European languages. Adapted from Anthony (2007), p 12.

which emphasises yet again the importance of cattle in ancient times. The words most frequently used reveal something of the lifestyle of those who spoke PIE. They suggest that 'the speakers of PIE inherited their rights and duties through the father's bloodline only (patrilineal descent); probably lived with the husband's family after marriage (patrilocal residence); recognised the authority of chiefs …; likely had formally instituted warrior bands; practiced ritual sacrifices of cattle and horses; drove wagons; recognized a male sky deity; …' [25]. A pretty androcentric culture, it seems to me. Moreover, this attitude endured. 'Kinship terms referring to grandfather, father, brother and husband's brother survive in clearly corresponding roots in nearly all Indo-European languages, whereas those relating to wife and wife's family are few, uncertain and variable' [26]. In short, 'the connection between animals, brothers, and power was the foundation on which new forms of male-centered ritual and politics developed among Indo-European-speaking societies' [27]. On the other hand the recent discovery of a female skeleton, dated to around 1700 BCE, with a silver diadem still attached to her forehead and other ornaments beside her in a grave at La Almoloya in southeastern Spain, suggests that 'one of the earliest European civilizations held some women in esteem' [28].

Indus Valley

Two great cities grew up here during the Bronze Age. The first was Harappa on the left bank of the Ravi, a tributary of the Indus. The second was Mohenjo-daro, 650 km downstream on the right bank of the Indus. The latter site is about 320 km northwest of present-day Karachi on the coast. The two cities and a thousand smaller settlements along the Indus constituted the Harappa people. According to archaeologist Sir Mortimer Wheeler, the '*idea* of civilization came to the Indus from the Euphrates and the Tigris, and gave the Harappa their initial direction or at least informed their purpose' [29]. Another active archaeologist of the Indus valley, Ernest Mackay, expressed a similar view: 'the regime was a theocracy, very similar in type to the contemporary theocracies of Sumer' [30]. But it had no temples, no palaces. In other ways, too, the Indus civilisation turned out rather differently to those in Mesopotamia, as I shall describe in a moment. At its height in 2500 BCE the civilisation encompassed an area larger than that of Sumer or Egypt. Although Harappa was the first city to be discovered and excavated, it is difficult to deduce much about the lifestyle of its people because its buildings, made of burnt brick, have in recent times become the source of material for new housing developments, as well as rubble for the construction of a railway line nearby. Mohenjo-daro has survived much better and has provided the bulk of information about the lives of the Harappa people over a period of 800 years. Some human skeletons unearthed at the lowest level (and therefore the oldest) show resemblance to skeletons recovered from Mesopotamia. It is therefore possible that both peoples had a common origin. The language spoken by the Harappa people is unknown. They had a pictographic script, but to date it has not been deciphered.

The Harappa do not appear to have been militant. No weapons of copper or bronze have been found, and they did not bother with a defensive wall. Although their cities were occasionally invaded by warring tribes from neighbouring Baluchistan to the west, these were successfully repulsed. The civilisation endured for 700 years from its height in 2600 BCE. Yet the Harappa abandoned the Indus valley during the 19th century BCE. If not because of subjugation by others, then why? The answer seems to lie with rising waters of the very river that had sustained them for so long. Historian and prolific author Andrew Robinson observes that 'my own hunch, for what it is worth, is that changes in the river systems of the Indus area accentuated existing weaknesses in the political structure of the Indus civilization and in due course undermined its unity and self-confidence' [31]. Certainly much of Mohenjo-daro today is under water, the river having risen by some 8 m. Many of the city's treasures — in stone and plaster, copper and bronze — undoubtedly lie beneath the waters. But much has been revealed.

Mohenjo-daro is the largest of the Harappa cities. The site today encompasses an area of 250 hectares, which is half that of Uruk. Harappa itself covers 150 hectares. The largest building in Mohenjo-daro appears to have been a kind of bath house, 'the earliest public water tank in the ancient world, a rectangle measuring 12 m by 7 m, with two wide staircases to the north and south leading down to a brick floor at max depth of 2.4 m, made watertight by a thick layer of bitumen' [32]. The city also had an extensive drainage system, as did Harappa. Their sanitary arrangements were 2,000 years ahead of such facilities in Rome. On the other hand its buildings lacked the splendour of those in Sumer, with no decorative features, no evidence of wall paintings and no life-size statues. A kind of austerity that reminds one of post-Reformation and Cromwellian England, though there is no evidence of previous grandeur in the case of the Indus civilisation. Mohenjo-daro did, however, have what may well have been the largest granary store in the ancient world. This should surprise no one, since 'the Indus civilization inevitably derived its wealth from a combination of agriculture and trade' [33].

The chief trade routes were to the north and to the west. The former was to the most northerly Indus settlement. This was Shortugai on the Oxus, situated near the lapis lazuli mines in northern Afghanistan. The westward route was to Mesopotamia, the chief trading partner. Stone weights indicate that goods were weighed. They were transported in wagons pulled by zebu cattle. No wagons have survived, but their use has been surmised from the number of children's toy carts in pottery that have been found. During the monsoon season the roads would have been impassable. So goods were transported by sea along the coast of the Arabian Sea. No forms of currency have been identified, but stone seals have been recovered along the main routes. Their significance is unknown. What is interesting about them is that such seals, and other objects, often depict a female goddess, reminiscent of the Mother Goddess of 'old Europe'. So perhaps an element of matriarchy survived among the Indus people. The 'importance of females as symbols of religious power is supported by the fact that figurines of women or mother goddesses are more common than male figurines' [34]. But there were also representations of male gods, several with animal accoutrements, such as an elephant's trunk. It has been suggested that such a figure may be the ancestor of the Hindu god Shiva, but there is little evidence for this.

The tenor of life in the valley of the Indus appears to have been more relaxed than that along the banks of the Euphrates. While the Sumerians were fighting Akkadian assailants, the Harappa were rolling dice and playing board games [35]. The former had powerful kings, palaces and temples, whereas the latter 'managed without kings, courts, military arms, palaces or public temples of any kind' [36]. Moreover, 'there was not much difference between the homes of rich and poor, no signs of differing diets in the bones of buried skeletons and no evidence of slavery' [37]. Might that have made it a little less androcentric, somewhat more favourable to women? The relatively austere buildings of the Harappa, compared with the opulence of Sumerian temples and palaces, reminds one again of Protestant rejection of Catholic iconography in England and northern Europe. Perhaps the Indus people were the world's first Reformers (though there was nothing to reform)?

Why they left the area is not clear. It was for good reason that the largest city was subsequently called Mohenjo-daro: 'city of the dead' in Sindi. After the collapse of the civilisation, new invaders from Iran arrived in 1500 BCE. They would settle throughout present day Pakistan, India, Bangladesh and other countries as far east as Chinese speakers across the Brahmaputra River. They were among the oldest speakers of Sanskrit and Persian, languages derived from the Indo-Iranian branch of the PIE language (Figure 3.2). They called themselves Aryan. Despite Western supremacists' fantasies — not only by the Nazis — the Aryans had nothing to do with the European people descended from the Baltic, Slavic, Germanic, Celtic, Italic, Albanian, Hellenic or Anatolian branches of the PIE speakers.

Nile Valley

No city in ancient Egypt could compare in extent or significance with those of Sumer or the Indus Valley. Neither Memphis in Lower Egypt nor Thebes in Upper Egypt were a match for Uruk or Ur, Harappa or Mohenjo-daro. But the Egyptians could boast of something different: the world's most experienced architects. One of these is said to have been Hemiunu, commissioned by King Khufu, Pharaoh of the Fourth Dynasty, to build the Great Pyramid at Giza near modern-day Cairo. Constructed around 2500 BCE, its four sides (each 230 m in length on the ground) are perfectly aligned on north–south and east–west axes. Until the spire on the central tower of Lincoln Cathedral was erected in 1311, it was the tallest building in the world. Khufu's reign lasted for well over 20 years, the time it took to complete the pyramid, so he may well have been interred there. The uncertainty arises from the fact that when the pyramid was entered during the 19th century, the sarcophagus within the 'king's chamber' was empty. Khufu's body has never been found.

In 1799 Napoleon invaded Egypt. One of his officers found a stone tablet near the town of Rashid. On it were three sets of inscriptions. The first was in the hieroglyphics that are on the walls of temples and tombs as well as on papyrus documents. The second was in an unknown script called demotic and known to have been used by the ordinary people. The third was in ancient Greek. This was easily translated and proved to be an edict issued in 196 BCE by Ptolemy V. The first two inscriptions seemed to be translations of the third, and opened the possibility of deciphering both. This was begun by Thomas Young in England. He then passed it to Jean François Champollion in France who completed the translation. As a result we know as much — if not more — about life in pharaonic Egypt as of that in Mesopotamia. The stone tablet, known as the Rosetta Stone after the site of its discovery, is now in the British Museum.

Egyptian society was strictly hierarchical. At the top were the gods, followed by the king who was considered divine as well as human. He was followed by his vizier. Next came the high priest of Amun, then other officials, down to the scribal class. All were male. Together they represented 1% of the population. The remainder, largely peasants and other workers, were illiterate. 'Because of their dominance men could perpetuate their control of the public, political sphere, while women, however able, could not officially gain entrance into the ruling bureaucracy' [38]. They did of course marry into the various classes but could not of themselves even become scribes. What did they do? Women married to the elite could own land and sell some of its produce. However, no merchant class, male or female, ever emerged in Egypt. Within their homes such women were known as 'mistress of the house'. They, or their female servants, would participate in baking, brewing and weaving. All other duties, such as labouring in the granary, looking after and butchering the cattle, and working in the carpenter's shop, would be carried out by men. Outside the home women were involved in similar occupations, as well as in performances of dance and music. They could also supervise the storage of food and cloths.

Some of these roles became restricted towards the end of the Old Kingdom (2150 BCE) and during the early years of the Middle Kingdom (2040 BCE onwards). 'It is difficult to avoid the impression that women of the Middle Kingdom were less frequently and significantly engaged in administering people and property than was previously the case ... not that their role was ever of great importance except, of course, in the case of mother, wife, or daughters of kings' [39]. Moreover, 'in the Old Kingdom it was possible for a woman to be an overseer of one of these troupes' of dancing, singing and clapping women, 'but by the Middle Kingdom this position of authority had passed to men' [40]. Life was becoming more androcentric.

Royal status was transmitted through the female line, in other words the queen. So in order to marry a royal offspring, the king married his sister, half-sister or daughter. Some of these unions may have been consummated, others not. Queens could rule as regents on behalf of their young sons, and several did so, especially when a dynasty came to its end. One queen, however, went further and decided to rule as king. This was Hatshepsut. She was the daughter of the Eighteenth Dynasty Thutmosis I (reigned 1504–1492) and half-sister (and wife — remember this is Pharaonic Egypt) of his son, Thutmosis II (1492–1479). When the latter died, his son became King Thutmosis III (1479–1425) [41]. Hatshepsut was named regent. She carried out her duties meticulously for a few years but her ambition got the better of her. She named herself king in 1473. In order to legitimise this act Hatshepsut had herself depicted on monuments dressed in male attire with the traditional beard. She proved to be a clever and successful ruler. An expedition down the Red Sea to the land of Punt (in present-day Sudan) brought back 31 live myrrh trees, frankincense, a panther, ostrich feathers, ivory, gold and other objects desired by the

Egyptians. It was said of her that 'God's Wife Hatchepsut (*sic*), governed Egypt and the Two Lands were under her control. People worked for her, and Egypt bowed her head' [42]. Thutmosis III tolerated Hatshepsut's rule well into his twenties, but after she died (or was assassinated) he obliterated all depictions of her as king (though not those showing her as Queen Regent). Another ambitious woman who ruled as pharaoh at the end of the Ptolemaic dynasty, of course, was Cleopatra. Having seduced Julius Caesar and borne him a son, she made one mistake that cost her, eventually, her life. At Caesar's death she chose the wrong Roman: Mark Anthony instead of Octavian, the future emperor Augustus.

This is an appropriate moment to recapitulate. In the opening chapter I showed that the physical differences between male and female — the former's stronger muscles, the latter's ability to give birth and nurture the newborn with empathy — do not affect their cerebral functions. Some males are indecisive and weak, some females resolute and strong. Some men never reach their potential, some women become effective rulers, inspired writers, brilliant scientists, incisive politicians. The chapters that follow will give examples of such women throughout the ages. So androcentrism does not depend on innate cerebral differences between male and female. It is an attitude based largely on culture, not biology. When, then, did it arise? I have taken the view that the emergence of hierarchies during the Neolithic and Bronze Ages was a major factor in the rise of gender inequality. Protecting cattle led to the advent of chiefs who were male, just as warriors were male due to their muscular superiority. The assumption that chiefs were a kind of warrior then led to the unjustified concept of male leadership. Kingship ensued. Some tasks, such as operating furnaces for the smelting of metals (unlike the moulding of pottery), do require masculine muscles. Other inequalities like the acquisition of property, social status or wealth were then assumed to be the preserve of men. This focus on the development of hierarchies to explain androcentrism has good precedent.

In 1884 Friedrich Engels, philosopher, political scientist and supporter (not least financially) of Karl Marx published a work titled *The Origin of the*

Family, Private Property and the State. In the chapter on *Barbarism and Civilization* he wrote, 'The distinction between rich and poor was added to that between free men and slaves. This and the new division of labor constitute a new division of society into classes' [43], in other words, hierarchies. In regard to the family, he wrote, 'The same cause that once had secured the supremacy in the house for women, viz. the confining of women's activity to domestic labor, now assured the supremacy of the men in the households', which included looking after cattle and other tamed animals; 'Man's advent to practical supremacy in the household marked the removal of the last barrier to his universal supremacy. His unlimited rule was emphasized and endowed with continuity by the downfall of matriarchy, the introduction of patriarchy, and the gradual transition from the pairing family to the monogamic family. ...' [43]. Engels clearly saw patriarchy as a cultural, not a biological, phenomenon. Moreover, he identified the period between 'barbarism' and 'civilisation', that approximates to the topic of this and the previous chapter, as a defining moment: the transgression from matriarchy (the 'old Europe' described by Marija Gimbutas) to androcentrism.

The French anthropologist and founder of structuralism, Claude Lévy-Strauss, also considered androcentrism not to be an innate phenomenon. But his explanation was rather different. Writing 80 years after Engels, he notes that 'the prohibition of incest is less a rule prohibiting marriage with the mother, sister, or daughter, than a rule obliging the mother, sister, or daughter to be given to others. It is the supreme rule of the gift.' [45]. Lévy-Strauss is talking about tribal societies and the exchange of women between them. He considers that viewing women as objects to be bartered is the essence of women's subordination, which led to the concept of private property — a sort of Engels in reverse. The American historian Gerda Lerner follows Lévy-Strauss. She considers that the 'development of agriculture in the Neolithic period fostered the inter-tribal "exchange of women", not only as a means of avoiding incessant warfare by the cementing of marriage alliances but also because societies with more women could produce more children' who would participate in agriculture and so 'increase production and accumulate surpluses' [46].

Moving on to the Bronze Age, Lerner notes that 'by the second millennium BC in Mesopotamian societies, the daughters of the poor were sold into marriage or prostitution in order to advance the economic interests of their families. The daughters of men of property could command a bride price, paid by the family of the groom to the family of the bride, which frequently enabled the bride's family to secure more financially advantageous marriages for their sons, thus improving the family's economic position' [47]. Lerner's conclusion is that 'the patriarchal family has been amazingly resilient and varied in different times and places. Oriental patriarchy encompassed polygamy and female enclosure in harems. Patriarchy in classical antiquity and in its European development was based upon monogamy, but in all its forms a double standard, which disadvantages women, was part of the system' [48]. I have tried to show, by different examples, how androcentrism in Europe, Asia and north Africa became firmly established during the Bronze Age.

Notes

1. Markin Metal Powders: http://www.makin-metals.com/about/history-of-bronze-infographic/
2. De Ryck *et al*: An overview of Mesopotamian bronze metallurgy during the 3rd millennium BC. *Journal of Cultural Heritage* **6**: 261–268 (2005).
3. Gimbutas (1965), p 21.
4. Ewen Callaway: Bronze age DNA hints at roots of social inequality. *Nature* **574**: 304–305 (2019).
5. Childe (1930), p 5.
6. from 'King Solomon's Mines', part of 'Ancient Mysteries', aired on the UK television channel 5 on 8 March 2020.
7. Hua Zhang *et al*: Osteoarthritis, labour division, and occupational specialization of the Late Shang China — insights from Yinxu (ca. 1250–1046 B.C.). *PLoS One* **12**: e0176329 (2017).
8. Coles and Harding (1979), p 535.
9. Nicola Crüsemann: *Uruk — 5,000 Years of the Megacity*, in Crüsemann *et al* (2019), p 12.
10. Crüsemann *et al* (2019), front end-paper map.

11. Guillermo Algaze: *The End of Prehistory and the Uruk Period*, in Crawford (2013), p 74.

12. Helga Vogel: *The 'Great Man of Uruk'. The Art of Governance in the Late Fourth and Early Third Millennia*, in Crüsemann *et al* (2019), p 124.

13. Tony J Wilkinson: *Hydraulic Landscapes and Irrigation Systems of Sumer*, in Crawford (2013), p 33 *et seq*.

14. Anthony (2007), pp 66–72.

15. Bond and Hempsell (2008).

16. Crawford (2013), pp xxiii and xxiv.

17. Claudia E Suter: *Kings and Queens: Representation and Reality*, in Crawford (2013), p 201.

18. *ibid*, p 203.

19. Julia M Asher-Greve: *Women and Agency: A Survey from Late Uruk to the End of Ur III*, in Crawford (2013), p 360.

20. *ibid*, p 368.

21. Enders (2020), p 1.

22. Robert McCormick Adams: *Heartland of Cities* (Chicago: Aldine, 1981), p xvii.

23. Anthony (2007), pp 27–30.

24. Oliver (2020), footnote on p 136.

25. Anthony (2007), p 15.

26. *ibid*, p 328.

27. *ibid*, p 138.

28. Vicente Lull *et al*: Emblems and spaces of power during the Argaric Bronze Age at La Almoloya, Murcia. *Antiquity* 95: 329–348 (2021).

29. Wheeler (1968), p 135.

30. Mackay (1948), p xiii.

31. Robinson (2015), p 143.

32. *ibid*, p 15.

33. Wheeler (1968), p 72.

34. Kenoyer (1998), p 134.

35. Mackay (1948), p 138.

36. Robinson (2015), p 106.

37. Andrew Robinson: Forgotten Utopia, *New Scientist* (17 Sep 2015), pp 31–33.

38. Robins (1993), p 19.

39. Henry G Fischer: *Egyptian Studies I: Varia* (New York: Metropolitan Museum of Art, 1976), p 79; quoted by Robins (1993), p 116.
40. Robins (1993), p 120.
41. such apparently precise dates, referring to people who lived thousands of years ago, are open to criticism. More accurate are the lifetimes and events that relate to a particular pharaoh. This is because inscriptions on temples and monuments describe episodes that were made during the life of such a person — identified by his *cartouche* or personal symbol. Thus, for example, 'King Thutmosis III died in his 54th year'.
42. Tyldesley (1994), p 222.
43. Engels (1902), p 198.
44. *ibid*, p 196.
45. Claude Lévy-Strauss: *The Elementary Structures of Kinship* (Boston: Beacon Press, 1969), p 481; quoted by Lerner (1986), p 24.
46. Lerner (1986), p 212.
47. *ibid*, p 213.
48. *ibid*, p 216.

Chapter 4

Maintenance: Classical Age Civilisations

The civilisations mentioned in the previous chapter had all come to an end by the time of the Christian era. In Mesopotamia the remnants of the Babylonian empire had expired by the middle of the 1st millennium BCE, in the Indus Valley even earlier, and pharaonic Egypt was now a Roman colony. But as one civilisation expires, another arises. The human thirst for innovation and repair is irrepressible [1]. Here I will discuss the civilisations that grew up in Persia and Europe, and the effect that androcentrism had on the lives of their women. However, 'almost all the literature of the ancient world was written by men; all the surviving artefacts, so far as we know, were made by men; women's lives are presented, if at all, from a man's point of view; the tiny proportion of work which is, or may be, by women does not tell us nearly enough about women's lives. Very few individual women are known to us, and much basic information about how women lived — let alone what they thought about it — is just not available. As if that were not enough, the information we have is, like all information from the ancient world, mostly about an elite' [2].

Persia

In the previous chapter I mentioned the Aryan speakers who entered the Indus Valley after the collapse of its civilisation. Their tribes spread across Iran (Persia) and present-day Afghanistan, Pakistan and India. Various nations, such as the Medes in the north and Persians in the rest of Iran, fought not only each other but also their neighbours in Mesopotamia. Eventually one man arose who united all of these and went on to establish the largest realm in the world. He was Cyrus the Great (*c* 600–530 BCE). The Achaemenid empire (approximately 550–330 BCE) that he founded encompassed Anatolia in the north, Egypt in the south, Afghanistan in the east, Mesopotamia in the west. To maintain order over such a vast area the Persians built roads that were sometimes no more than a track across mountains. The major route was the Khorasan Highway. This ran from the headwaters of the Indus in the east to Babylon in the west, with a further section into Lydia on the western shore of Anatolia [3]. A postal service, perhaps the first in the world, provided communication between major towns. After Alexander the Great's Asian conquests, his supporters, the Seleucids, ruled over Persia for some 60 years, followed by Parthians from the east. Stability was restored under the Sasanian dynasty (224–651 CE), that was terminated by Muslim invaders from Arabia.

Much of our knowledge about life during Achaemenid times is derived from two sources: tablets from the capital Persepolis that survived Alexander's wanton destruction, and Greek authors. The two often represent different points of view. This is hardly surprising in that Persia was Greece's greatest enemy. For a decade (490–480 BCE) the mighty Persian forces had been attacking solitary Athens until its citizens (supported by ships from Sparta and other city states) finally saw the invader off for good.

Historian Maria Brosius has made a study of women's lives during Achaemenid times. At the top of the hierarchy was the king's mother. Although she exercised no political power, she was able to further the interests of family members and could intercede with the king if the life of one of the court ladies was in jeopardy. Next came the king's wife, followed by his daughters. The king's concubines — who could number over 300 — came mainly from non-Persian families. In that way they differed from the rest of the court who had to be of Persian descent. During the day concubines might join the king's hunt. At night they 'guarded his sleep, singing and playing music' [4]. Satraps or regional governors, as well as wealthy men outside the court, were allowed to own concubines.

From administrative details recorded during the reign of Darius I (who usurped the throne in 522 BCE) on tablets known as the Persepolis Foundation texts, Brosius has deciphered what royal women were able to do. To begin with, they could own land — whole villages even — on which they were taxed. But they could recoup this by selling the grain and other produce from the fields. They gave orders to their staff (male and female) and were obeyed at all times. Workers, including female overseers, received a ration of food and wine. This was generally the same for male and female staff unless their jobs were different. A woman controlling a workforce of 161 individuals might receive 50 quarts (47.3 litres) of grain, 30 quarts of wine and 4 sheep a year. The workers themselves were typically awarded 20 or 30 quarts of grain and 10 or 20 quarts of wine. Mothers, it should be noted, received special rations. Much of the work carried out by women concerned agricultural products that were stored in granaries. The royal granary at Persepolis, for example, held 8,000 quarts of flour. As in Egypt, however, women could not become scribes. Brosius concludes her account by pointing out that 'it is unthinkable to continue holding the view that the women at the Achaemenid court were only an undifferentiated mass leading a life behind palace walls without any function and purpose' [5].

Indeed, and not only royal women. The best-known businesswoman, who lived during the reign of Darius I, was one Irdabama. She supervised a workforce of 480 people. Her trading business took her to the farthest corners of the Achaemenid empire: Babylon in the west, Syria to the north, Egypt to the south. While there are few records of businesswomen during the Parthian period, the freedom that women had enjoyed during Achaemenid times was sustained — even increased — during the Sassanid period.

Another role to which some women were able to aspire was, surprisingly, the military. Three notable women fought bravely but, as it happens, in battles that were eventually lost. Artemesia I of Caria served as an admiral under Xerxes I at Salamis in 480 BCE. Although this sea battle was won by the Greeks, Artemesia had the privilege of escorting Xerxes' sons back home. During the Parthian time, King Artabanus IV appointed his daughter Sura to lead his troops against the invading forces of Ardashir I. The latter prevailed and the Parthian empire gave way to the Sassanid. That dynasty ruled successfully for more than 400 years until Arab forces under Caliph Umar ibn Al-Khattab arrived at its border. Over the next five years the invading Muslims won battle after battle against the dispirited Sassanids. At one point the invaders were confronted by troops under the command of a woman, Apranik by name. Although her force was defeated, she refused to surrender. Instead, she organised guerrilla attacks on the enemy until she was finally killed in battle. It is but one instance of many showing that, given the opportunity, women can exhibit bravery as well as any man [6]. I will describe the exploits of two other feisty women towards the end of this chapter.

In contrast to practice in pharaonic Egypt, kingship was not associated with a deity. The god Ahura Mazda (Wise Lord) was worshipped alike by the king and his subjects. Ahura Mazda is the creator of the world, and the major figure of Zoroastrianism. The religion was founded by Zoroaster (Zarathustra), a prophet who probably lived in 7th century BCE Persia. Since Zoroastrianism is practiced in Iran and elsewhere to this day, it can claim to be one of the oldest religions of the world alongside Judaism, Hinduism, Buddhism and Confucianism. Might not the relative tolerance of women in the Zoroastrian faith have contributed towards the opportunities for women of ancient Persia to lead lives not entirely subservient to men?

Greece

The Greeks 'looked at the relations between the two sexes from a point of view utterly strange to us. Amongst us there exists a clear and definite doctrine which lays down rigidly what is right and what is wrong. The Greeks had no such doctrine. … They did not feel or think that one definite course of conduct was right, and the other wrong; but they had to judge in each case whether the action was becoming, whether it was in harmony with the nobler side of human nature, whether it was beautiful or useful' [7]. A singular case of androcentrism, or rather two, as I shall describe.

Greek (Minoan) culture began at Knossos on the island of Crete around 2000 BCE and ended in Athens when the Ottoman Turks bombarded the Parthenon in 1458 CE. Athens was but one of several city-states that had grown up within the Mycenaean civilisation. The dominant one was, by around 650 BCE, Sparta. Situated in the southeast of the Peloponnese peninsula, it was a self-governing state. The kings who had ruled were now no more than figureheads or generals in the army. Power lay in the hands of a council of elders who controlled every aspect of life. As far as women were concerned, they had but one function: to produce healthy children. In order to achieve this, all girls had to participate in gymnastic exercises and competitions with each other. This included wrestling, running, and throwing the quoit and javelin. It has been suggested that they competed in these sports with boys (both sexes devoid of clothing). It was then incumbent on girls, as well as on young men, to marry. But if she was in any way not in perfect health she could not only avoid marriage, she was forbidden from marrying altogether. In order to produce perfect offspring, an unhealthy or malformed child was disposed of. The result was that 'for about four or five hundred years there was a succession of the strongest men that possibly ever existed on the face of the earth' [8]. It was the earliest, and fortunately the only (except for attempts by the Nazis during the 1930s and 40s), eugenics project. Since men were subject to the same constraints as women, the regime was rather more authoritative than androcentric. It was criticised by Aristotle only for allowing women to own most of the property. In fact they owned 40% of Spartan land. Elsewhere (apart from Athens), women had even more control: they could own houses, land and slaves, and could enter into mortgages and loans.

Athens became the largest of the city-states by the 6th century BCE. 'There was one class' of Athenian women 'who could scarcely move a step from their own room and who were watched and restricted in every possible way. There was another class on whom no restrictions whatever were laid, who could move about and do whatever seemed good in their own eyes' [9]. The first class had, like Spartan women, one duty: to marry — at 15 or 16 years of age — and produce healthy children. Since they were not expected to concern themselves with intellectual matters, education of girls was minimal. Women did not own property. Athenian men were content with docile wives. If they wished to discuss higher matters, they could do so at a social function (from which Athenian women were largely excluded) with women of the second class: foreigners. Many of these women, who were not Athenian citizens, were well educated. They dabbled in the arts and science, in philosophy and politics: they could satisfy their 'hunger of the mind' [10]. Some married, others not. If their relationships were occasionally haphazard, there was no impropriety in regard to their friendship with male citizens. The latter enjoyed their company solely for stimulating conversation.

One such lady was Theodota. When she arrived in Athens she sought out Socrates who, according to Xenophon, was delighted to discuss her art with her. The best known foreigner who arrived in Athens was Aspasia of Miletus. Well educated and said to be attractive if not beautiful, Pericles fell for her. His marriage was not going well, and by mutual consent he and his wife divorced. Aspasia moved in. As an Athenian citizen Pericles could not marry her. But they had a happy life together. She founded a renowned school for girls and became the focus of intellectual and artistic life in Athens. To her salon came Euripides and Sophocles, Plato and Socrates. The latter even called her his teacher. Being famous and well regarded, it is not surprising that scurrilous stories about her circulated. On Pericles' death, Aspasia married Lysicles, a sheep merchant, whom she propelled into one of the most prominent positions in Athens. She reminds me somewhat of Mme de Staël (see chapter 6).

Plato, in the *Republic*, considered women to be as 'capable of showing the same moral qualities as men, and that natural ability occurs regardless of sex' though he thought that 'most women were less able than most men'. But he and Socrates were alone in promoting the education of women. In contrast Aristotle regarded women as 'a defective kind of human' [11] and that 'subjugation of women was both "natural" and a "social necessity"' [12]. Either way, 'though there never was in the history of the world such a numerous race of great thinkers, poets, sculptors, painters and architects, in one city at one time as in Athens, not one Athenian woman ever attained to the slightest distinction in any one department of literature, art, or science' [13]. Perhaps, but as I have indicated, there were non–Athenian women who came up to the mark.

One who studied in Plato's Academy was Arete of Cyrene (~370–340 BCE). 'She was the daughter of Aristippus, founder of the Cyrenaic School of philosophy. Arete was elected to succeed her father as head of the school. She is said to have taught natural science, moral philosophy and ethics in Attica for 35 years, and to have written at least 40 books, including treatises on Socrates, agriculture and education. Her pupils included some 110 philosophers' [14]. Then there was 4th century BCE Hipparchia of Thessaly. She married the Cynic philosopher Krates, but apart from a clever remark made at a dinner party she passes 'out of history, still asserting that she was right to prefer philosophy to weaving' [15].

With regard to female writers, American classicist Ellen Greene lists over 30 [16]. One was the poet **Sappho**, born on the Greek island of Lesbos around 630 BCE. She is said to have run a school for girls but the occupation at which she excelled was writing lyric poetry. Some of her compositions were likely sung to the accompaniment of music [17]. Fragments of poetry on papyri that were discovered at Fayum in Egypt in the 19th century are said to be her work. She wrote throughout her life, which spanned more than 60 years. However, over 90% of what she is assumed to have composed, and that was known to early publishers in Athens and Alexandria, has been lost. Sappho is known for the nature of her private life. The word 'sapphic' was used 100 years ago by writers such as Virginia Woolf as an earlier version of today's 'lesbian'. During her time Sappho was credited with giving birth to a daughter Cleis and to have died by throwing herself off a rock for the love of a ferryman. None of this, of course, is incompatible with an unconventional lifestyle, and it so happens that her only complete poem to have survived is an *Ode to Aphrodite*. My reason for mentioning her is that 'she was the only woman in all antiquity whose productions by universal consent placed her on the same level with the greatest poets of the other sex' [18].

Returning to female philosophers, one who left a well-earned legacy did not live in Greece either and she was not even born until the second half of the 4th century CE, by which time Greece was a Roman colony. But

Hypatia of Alexandria was 'the most popular Greek philosopher ever —
trailing only Plato, Socrates, Aristotle and Pythagoras' [19]. Hypatia taught
in the mathematics school of her father Theon, whom she soon outshone,
rather like the young Mozart and his father Leopold. Although a brilliant
mathematician, it was Hypatia's philosophical ideas that particularly
attracted students to her school, and Alexandrians to her public discourses.
She was a Neoplatonist who tried to combine Plato's divine 'demi-urge'
and Greek paganism with recently arrived Christianity. To her, each was
equally valid. But not to others. Wearing as usual her philosopher's *tribon*
cloak, that alone annoyed many an androcentric Alexandrian, she was
attacked in the street by a band of fanatical Christian clerics. They dragged
her to the Caesareum church where she was stripped naked, torn limb from
limb, and set on fire. Her crime? Teaching pagan philosophy alongside
Christian doctrine. But mainly, I suspect, for being an intelligent and successful woman in a man's world.

In Athens, order had originally been maintained by kings. They were
succeeded by powerful statesmen. However, in 508 BCE the Athenians
came to the conclusion that a fairer form of government would be by
elected members of the people themselves: democracy was born. Its ideals
were summarised by Pericles when he delivered the first of annual Funeral
Orations on behalf of the fallen during the Peloponnesian War in 431 BCE.
It is such an eloquent description of democracy (said to have been written
in part by Aspasia) that I shall quote the relevant parts: 'If we look to the
laws, they afford equal justice to all in their private differences ... if a man
is able to serve the state, he is not hindered by the obscurity of his condition.
The freedom we enjoy in our government extends also to our ordinary life.
There, far from exercising a jealous surveillance over each other, we do not
feel called upon to be angry with our neighbour for doing what he likes ...
We throw open our city to the world, and never by alien acts exclude foreigners from any opportunity of learning or observing, although the eyes of
an enemy may occasionally profit by our liberality ... advancement in public life falls to reputations for capacity, class considerations not being
allowed to interfere with merit ... our ordinary citizens, though occupied
with the pursuits of industry, are still fair judges of public matters ... at

Athens we live exactly as we please, and yet are just as ready to encounter every legitimate danger ...' [20].

Apart from its adoption by Rome (until imperial rule was established in 27 BCE), the concept of democracy lay dormant for more than 1,000 years. It was resurrected in 1648 by Switzerland and towards the end of the 18th century by the United States of America and the newly established Republic of France (chapter 6). The democratic principle has eventually been followed by most countries in the world. But until the 20th century, as in ancient Athens, voting was restricted to males.

Rome

The seat of power in a civilisation often does not remain in the same place. In Egypt it moved from Memphis (near modern Cairo) to Thebes, to Alexandria and eventually back to Cairo. In Persia the capital was Babylon, followed by Persepolis during the Achaemenid period, Ctesiphon in Parthian and Sasanian times, and Tehran since the late 18th century. But the history of the Romans began in Rome in the 7th century BCE and ended there 1,000 years later. During that time it grew into the largest empire of its day, spanning three continents, and is still the capital of the Italians. For good reason has it been called the Eternal City. What were the reasons for its success? From the beginning of the Republic in the 5th century BCE to its end in 27 BCE, Romans espoused the rule of law, promoted culture and sustained democracy. Even when ultimate power had passed to the emperor, the rights of Roman citizens were protected. As far as women were concerned, male superiority was assumed at all times.

Roman women were, like female Athenian citizens, expected to marry and produce children. They were also kept out of politics. No Roman woman ever set foot in the Senate, or had a vote. On the other hand they had more of a social life, like Athenian foreign women, and dined out in the company of men. With them they discussed politics and the arts. 12 known female poets (though fewer than in Athens) are listed by Ellen Greene [16]. A Roman woman did not take her husband's name, and could, after her father's death, own property that she could dispose of at her will.

Occasionally a group of determined and vocal women could cause the Senate to change its mind over a particular issue. During the Republic a woman could sit with her husband in the amphitheatre, but Augustus relegated women to the back (as became the norm in synagogues and mosques). Divorce, generally at the husband's instigation of course, was common. 'It is said that Ovid and Pliny the younger married three times, Caesar and Antony four times, Sulla and Pompey five times; Juvenal talks of a woman having married eight husbands in five years, and Martial of a woman being married to her tenth husband' [21].

The town of Pompeii, at the foot of Mount Vesuvius near Naples, gives us a special insight to life during the 1st century CE. The eruption of Vesuvius in 79, that was 100,000 times more powerful than the atomic bombs dropped on Hiroshima and Nagasaki during the second world war, released molten rock and ash at 1.5 million tons per second. These buried the town in a frozen state until serious excavations began during the 18th century and continued thereafter. From the type of buildings that existed, historian Mary Beard has deduced the kind of life led by its inhabitants [22]. The town appears to have contained a few thousand Roman men. This extrapolates to a population of at least ten times that number to include women, children and slaves.

Apart from going to the bath house and rearing children, what else could women do? If wealthy, they could finance the erection of public buildings. One of the largest, with a wide courtyard, was called the Building of Eumachia to reflect the name of its donor. She came from one of the leading families and was actually a priestess. Another major building was sponsored by one Mamia, also a priestess. The number of occupations a woman could decently undertake was limited. But there are records of one woman, a former slave called Nigella who was designated as a 'public pig keeper', and another, Faustilla, who ran a small pawnbroker business [23].

Most of the baths had separate entrances, changing rooms, and warm and hot plunges for the two sexes. The courtyard where people could stroll, exercise and meet after the bath was common ground. Naturally the bath water was not disinfected, nor changed too frequently. 'The hot tubs in the bathing suite itself must have been a seething mass of bacteria ... Martial jokes about the faeces that ended up in them, and the Roman medical writer Celsus offers the sensible advice not to go to the baths with a fresh wound ("it normally leads to gangrene"). The baths, in other words, may have been a place of wonder, pleasure and beauty for the humble Pompeian bather. They might also have killed him' [24]. Near the outskirts of the town was a bathhouse without separate sections for men and women. Here, it seems, bathing was not the only activity. To describe it as a brothel would not be an overstatement.

What of life elsewhere? The Vestal Virgins were a small group of women, named after the virgin Roman goddess Vesta, who remained single. Their 'religious duties fitted into the family and civic setting, except in that they gave women an acknowledged public status and activity' [25]. The advent of Christianity gradually reduced the opportunities that Roman women in general had acquired. '… at the very first stage women take a prominent part in the spread of Christianity … but in a short time women are seen only in two capacities: as martyrs and deaconesses' [26]. The role of a deaconess was not arduous: to stand outside the building dedicated to Christian worship and direct the congregation to their seats.

Two determined and courageous women, neither a Roman and both living on the periphery of the empire, distinguished themselves by giving the mighty Roman army a bloody nose. **Boudica** (Boadicea during my school days) is known for inciting a revolt against the Roman occupiers of Britain during 60–61 CE. Although Julius Caeasr had invaded Britain in 55 BCE and again a year later, he did not stay to subjugate the inhabitants. It was the emperor Claudius who achieved this by sending an army of 40,000 across the Channel in 43 CE. Most of England and Wales were conquered. For more than 15 years the indigenous tribes succumbed to Roman rule. But when the provincial governor Suetonius Paulinus was in Anglesey with the army in order to suppress a Druid revolt, Boudica seized the opportunity to attack the invaders. Our knowledge of what followed is based largely on the writings of Tacitus and Cassius Dio. The former was born in Provence in 56 or 57. The latter in Bithynia, a Roman province in northwest Turkey, around 150. So neither was present when the uprising took place. Not surprisingly their accounts differ in several regards. Worse than that, Tacitus wrote two accounts, one in the late 90s and another between 115 and 117. The first is the *Agricola*, largely a biography of his father-in-law Julius Agricola. He was a Roman official in Britain during the revolt, becoming governor of the province some time later. The second work, the *Annals*, is a history of the Roman Empire between 14 and 68. This contradicts the first in several places. So the reader will appreciate that knowledge of events that took place 2,000 years ago, even when written records have survived, is generally uncertain.

Boudica was the wife of the king of the Iceni, one Prasutagus, who was actually very friendly towards the Romans (not blessed with a son, he made the emperor Claudius co-heir with his two daughters). But he would die before the revolt took place. The Iceni occupied most of present-day Norfolk, as well as parts of Suffolk, Cambridgeshire, Essex and East Leicestershire. In the *Agricola*, Tacitus explains the frustration of the natives: 'We gain nothing by submission except heavier burdens for willing shoulders. Once each tribe had one king, now two are clamped on us — the legate [Suetonius Paulinus] to reap his fury on our lives, the procurator [Catus Decianus, responsible for taxing the province] on our property' [27]. Boudica appears to have been listening. According to Tacitus in the *Annals*, 'Boudica drove round all the tribes in a chariot with her daughters in front of her. "We British are used to woman commanders in war", she cried. "I am descended from mighty men. But now I am not fighting for my kingdom and wealth. I am fighting as an ordinary person for my lost freedom, my bruised body, and my outraged daughters. ... Consider how many of you are fighting — and why. Then you will win this battle, or perish. That is what I, a woman, plan to do! — let the men live in slavery if they will."' [28].

'Goaded by such mutual encouragements, the whole island rose under the leadership of Boudicca (*sic*), a lady of royal descent — for Britons make no distinction of sex in their leaders. ... They hunted down the Roman troops in their scattered posts, stormed the forts and assaulted the colony itself in which they saw their slavery focussed ...' [29]. In fact the whole island did not rise up. It was the Iceni, supported by their southerly neighbours the Trinobantes and a few others, who instigated the revolt. (Elsewhere in the *Agricola* Tacitus places Boudica as leading the Brigantes, a tribe south of the Scottish border. But the Brigantes, whose leader was another woman, Cartimandua, did not, as far as we know, participate in the revolt.) Suetonius Paulinus, on hearing of the revolt, quickly returned from Anglesey. In the *Annals* Tacitus reports that 'kingdom and household alike were plundered like prizes of war, the one by Roman officers, the other by Roman slaves. As a beginning, his [Prasutagus'] widow Boudica was flogged and their daughters raped. The Icenian chiefs were deprived of their hereditary estates as if the Romans had been given the whole country. The king's own relatives were treated like slaves.' [30]. Things got even nastier as Suetonius decided that the Britons should be further reminded of the error of their ways. 'Suetonius, undismayed, marched through disaffected territory to Londinium', then no more than a large village. He 'decided to sacrifice the single city of Londinium to save the province as a whole. ... Suetonius gave the signal for departure. The inhabitants were allowed to accompany him. But those who stayed because they were women, or old, or attached to the place, were slaughtered by the enemy. Verulamiun [St Albans] suffered the same fate' [31].

The words that Cassius Dio puts in Boudica's mouth are strangely similar to those attributed to her by Tacitus. 'You have learned by actual experience how different freedom is from slavery. ... (You) have been deceived by the alluring promises of the Romans, yet now that you have tried both, how great a mistake you made in preferring an imported despotism to your ancestral mode of life, and you have come to realise how much better is poverty with no master than wealth with slavery' [32]. On other details of the revolt they differ. '... a terrible disaster occurred in Britain. Two cities were sacked, 80,000 of the Romans and of their allies perished and the island was lost to Rome' [33]. According to Tacitus almost 80,000 of the insurgents were killed, with 400 Romans dead. Both references to 80,000 are probably a gross overestimate. What Dio means by the island being 'lost to Rome' is not clear. The Romans remained in Britain throughout Dio's lifetime and would continue to do so for almost two centuries after his death. According to Tacitus, Boudica poisoned herself. Dio asserts that she fell ill, died and was given a royal burial (the site of which has eluded archaeologists to this day). Take your pick.

The other woman who defied the Roman might was **Zenobia** (*c* 240–274 CE), queen of the Syrians. She was 'determined, proud, ambitious and combative' according to one biographer, 'one of the most remarkable figures in the entire history of the Roman and Byzantine Near East' by another, and 'a most infamous adversary of Rome' by a third [34]. At 17 or 18 (some say 14) years of age she became the (second) wife of Odenathus (Odainat), who had proclaimed himself king of the Palmyrenes. The desert town of Palmyra had become an important centre for trade between Anatolia and Egypt, the Mediterranean and Persia. Ostensibly within the Roman empire, the Palmyrenes under Odenathus had developed delusions of independence. The young queen shared these with gusto. She was also something of an intellectual. Well-educated in philosophy and fluent in three languages (Greek, Egyptian and the local version of Aramaic), she could hold her own against any man. Dutifully she also bore Odenathus several children.

The empire had been humiliated by the capture of its emperor, Vespasian, in a botched attempt to conquer the Persians in 260. Odenathus took advantage of this and decided to snatch a bit of Persia for himself (or at least on behalf of Rome). Accompanied by Roman legions who were in no position to refuse, Odenathus drove the Sassanid emperor Shapur I eastward across the Euphrates. By 262 he was at the gates of Ctesiphon, on the left bank of the Tigris, south of present-day Baghdad. The city held out but the lands to the west fell to the Palmyrenes. Intoxicated by his success Odenathus took his army north into Anatolia to crush an attempted invasion by Germanic tribes. But his luck had run out and in 271 he was assassinated together with the son of his first marriage. At least three different versions of the perpetrators have been proposed. Back in Palmyra, Zenobia became regent on behalf of their eldest (10-year-old) son Vaballathus, and effective ruler of Palmyra. She had already decided, apparently while Odenathus was on campaign, to wrest Egypt from Roman control. According to author Yasmine Zahran, 'I occupied Antioch in 268 ... There was no resistance in the rest of Syria, as both the Pan-Hellenists and the native Semites rallied to my side, relieved to be rid of the Romans ... At the head of my army, with Zabadas, the chief commander at my side, I swept through Palestine ... and crashed through the provinces of Arabia. ... The conquest of Egypt was easy ... owing to the discontent of the Egyptians, and their exploitation by the Romans for three centuries ... to the Alexandrians I was the descendant of Cleopatra ...' [35].

But Zenobia's fortune would not last any longer than that of Odenathus. In 270 Aurelian, a battle-hardened cavalryman, became emperor. Two years later he turned his attention to restoring Roman supremacy in Syria. He advanced on Palmyra, where the defenders were spurred on by their queen. They fought the Romans as hard as they were able, but eventually were overcome by the skill and weaponry of the smaller invading force. Zenobia fled eastwards towards the Euphrates and was about to embark on a boat for safety when Aurelian's men captured her. Two versions of Zenobia's end are even more disparate than those relating to Boudica. In that of Aurelius Victor's *Historica Augusta* written around 395, 'Aurelian reprieved Zenobia, and carried her to Rome where she appeared in his triumphal procession in gold chains. He also gave her a villa and a Roman husband.' In his history of the Roman Empire written at the end of the 5th century, the Greek historian Zosimus states that 'Zenobia died on her way to Rome by illness or suicide by starvation' [36].

Elsewhere

During the Qin dynasty (pronounced *chin*, hence China) the warring tribes of different regions were conquered and united under the first Chinese emperor, Qin Shi Huang (259–210 BCE). Qin was interred together with his terracotta army of 8,000 soldiers and 670 horses near Xi'an in central China. The emperor clearly valued military protection over female company for his afterlife. The teachings of Confucius (591–479 BCE) had been adopted by the preceding dynasties of the Shang and the Zhou. Confucius instructed a woman to obey her father, then her husband, and after his death, her son. She should also be silent on most matters. Confucianism — a philosophy more than a religion — couldn't be more androcentric. It was suppressed under the Qin emperor, to be replaced by even more authoritative strictures. Confucianism was restored under the Han dynasty

(205 BCE to 220 CE) and has remained central to Chinese philosophical beliefs throughout the ages. Mao Zedong (1893–1976), founder of the Chinese Communist Party, was a strong proponent of Confucianism. But some of the non-Han (Chinese) people, like the Lahu of southwest China, are not at all androcentric even today: their society is essentially gender neutral [37].

In India, the Maurya Empire (322–185 BCE) covered the entire sub-continent, except the extreme south. It was brought to its peak by its emperor Ashoka (304–232 BCE). He espoused the teaching of Gautama Buddha (*c* 5th–4th century BCE). This holds that 'the establishment of the male principle in equal measure with the female principle is the natural order of things. They should never exist in a mutually exclusive relationship. They should not be an emphasis on one at the expense of the other, for both are indispensable' [38]. It is surely the only gender-neutral doctrine in the world. More than that, it is the only creed that does not condone slavery, which has been a feature of every civilisation that ever arose.

'It is one of the curious features of early Christianity that ... no objection is taken to slavery, though the Therapeutae had already denounced it as unlawful and inhuman' [39]. But the Therapeutae were probably a group of philosophers who followed Buddhism. So far as early Christianity is concerned, Christian doctrine is conspicuous by exhibiting more or less the same indifference to slavery right up to the early 19th century. And when, finally, the proponents of abolition in England, led by William Wilberforce (1759–1833), cited Christian values in support of their argument, the anti-abolitionists responded by using the same source to support theirs. Wilberforce lived to see the Act abolishing slavery in the British Empire passed by the Houses of Parliament. He had campaigned for this most of his life. Three days later he died.

Beliefs and Religions

Pagan beliefs and the religions that followed track cultural practices fairly well. Thus the Mother Goddess of old Europe during Neolithic times was succeeded by male creators during the Bronze Age. Ahura Mazda was male, as were the chief gods of the Egyptians and Greeks, although the latter two were accompanied by an equal number of female deities. The Romans adopted the Greek gods, as they did much of Greek culture, pausing only to give the gods Latin names: Zeus becomes Jove, Athena is Minerva, and so on. The monotheistic religions of Judaism, Christianity and Islam (that emerged in the 7th century CE) have a male creator at their head. While Christianity adapted the androcentric Jewish Torah into its Old Testament, the Gospels of the New Testament are more favourable to women. The two Marys — the mother of Jesus and the Magdalene — play notable roles in the Christian story. The chief practitioners of the three Abrahamic religions, however, have been male for two millennia. Only in recent times has non–Catholic (Anglican) Christianity adopted female deacons, priests, eventually bishops, and Reform Judaism recognised female rabbis. We're still waiting for a female imam.

Dark clouds hovered over most women during the Classical Age, as they had over those of previous times. Only occasionally did the clouds part to let in light. They did so for court ladies in Achaemenid Persia; for foreign women in Athens; for most Spartan women; and for many Roman matrons. As Christianity became established during the early years of the Middle Ages, another chink of light opened for women. Through the establishment of monasteries even non–elite women could find their voice. This is described in the following chapter.

Notes

1. Pasternak (2003).
2. Clark (1989), p 1.
3. Holland (2005), pp xvi and xvii.
4. Brosius (1996), p 31.
5. *ibid*, p 200.
6. Joshua J Mark: Women in Ancient Persia, *Ancient History Encyclopedia*. Last modified January 30, 2020. https://www.ancient.eu/article/1492/
7. Donaldson (1907), p 3.

8. *ibid*, p 29.
9. *ibid*, p 49.
10. Maria Mitchell: *A Hunger of the Mind* (London: Alembic Rare Books, 2019).
11. Clark (1989), p 5.
12. Power (2015), p 17.
13. Donaldson (1907), p 55.
14. Alic (1986), p 26.
15. Clark (1989), p 28.
16. Greene (2005), p 192 *et seq.*
17. Freeman (2016).
18. Donaldson (1907), p 41.
19. Watts (2017), p 4.
20. from Thucydides' *History of the Peloponnesian War*, available in English at the Perseus Project of Tufts University, MA, USA.
21. Donaldson (1907), p 117.
22. Beard (2008).
23. *ibid*, pp 168 and 169.
24. *ibid*, p 247.
25. Clark (1989), p 34.
26. Donaldson (1907), p 154.
27. Hingley and Unwin (2005), p 44.
28. *ibid*, p 50.
29. *ibid*, p 45.
30. *ibid*, p 47.
31. *ibid*, p 49.
32. *ibid*, p 56.
33. *ibid*, p 53.
34. quoted by Winsbury (2010), p 14.
35. Zahran (2003), p 29.
36. *ibid*, p 15.
37. see Shanshan Du: *Chopsticks Only Work in Pairs: Gender Unity and Gender Equality Among the Lahu of Southwestern China* (New York: Columbia University Press, 2002).
38. Ueki (2001), p 191.
39. Donaldson (1907), p 167.

Chapter 5

Easing: The Middle Ages

The Middle Ages in Europe [1] are thought to have been a period that was relatively more favourable to women than those before or after. For women the Dark Age, as the period is sometimes referred to, was suffused with a ray of light. This is by no means a majority view. Nevertheless I have decided to adopt it. What led to this easing? A major cause was surely the rise of Christianity. Hindus worship both male and female deities. Within the monotheistic religion of Abraham, Jews revere the male God Yaweh, Muslims pray to Allah and revere the prophet Mohammed. But for Christians, a separate focus is on Mary, the Mother of God. She is venerated almost as much as the God the Father, God the Son and the Holy Spirit. It is the human, not the spiritual, side of God that Mary the Virgin, and Mary Magdalene (for an opposite reason), represent. Christian men were aware of the distinction and in medieval times began to acknowledge this aspect of femininity. Women, after all, were responsible for their very birth. So a concept of 'Jesus as Mother' arose [2].

It was during the Middle Ages that monasteries began to emerge. From Egypt during the 4th century, the idea of monasticism spread north westwards into Europe. By the 6th century St Benedict of Nursia had written what he called 'a little rule for beginners' for the community he had founded at Monte Cassino, south of Rome, and this rule gradually spread to communities across Europe [3].

The earliest monastic houses for women (nowadays generally referred to as convents) were in France and Belgium. A monastic community that was divided into male and female houses was established on an island off Cannes around 400, followed by a similar one in Marseilles a decade later.

As far as we know, 8 houses for women (and 100 for men) had been established by around 550. The numbers grew steadily so that by 1100 there were 223 houses for women (compared with 2,599 for men). England followed this trend. Two convents were established in the 7th century: one in Lyminge in 633 and one in Folkestone at about the same time. By 650 there were 9 houses for women and 20 for men. The numbers had risen to 76 and 250 respectively by 1100. All the above figures should be taken with a pinch of salt. Their author calls them 'rough statistics of new religious foundations' which 'indicate that during the seventh century, a particular set of conditions prevalent in Frankish Gaul and Anglo–Saxon England fostered the development of monastic life for women' [4]. The greater opportunities for a cloistered life on the continent meant that many aspiring nuns joined their sisters there. However, it was not to last. Over the next 400 years, invading Saracens in France and Viking incursions into England decimated these religious sanctuaries. But the point had been made, and after the 12th century new monasteries for women began to reappear.

The 7th century may have improved one aspect of women's lives in Europe, but in Arabia a new religion — the third of the Abrahamic trio — was incubating. It would spread westwards across North Africa and into Spain as far as the Pyrenees. Eastwards it would reach Persia and be carried by the Ghurid emperors into India. Its tenets would curtail the lives of Muslim women for 1,300 years and counting. The cloister spawned poetry and music, religious tracts and philosophy. In the harem, future rulers were born (the concept of separate living quarters for the wives and concubines of a monarch actually goes back to pharaonic times in Egypt).

So far as the ability of Muslim women to lead their own lives during the Middle Ages is concerned, there are plenty of examples. Umm al-Darda was a 7th-century lawyer living in Baghdad. In journalist Carla Power's words, 'I've tried to worship Allah in every way but I've never found a better one than sitting around debating other scholars' [5]. Another jurist was Fatima al-Fahri, the daughter of a wealthy merchant, born in Tunisia. She moved with him to Fez where she is said to have founded the Quarawiyyin mosque in 859. Its madrasa became the University of al-Quarawiyy in 1963, and the unbroken function of the mosque as a seat of learning has led to it being considered the oldest university in the world [6]. Mariam al-Astrulabiyy was a 10th-century astronomer from Aleppo. Her name derives from the fact that she was a renowned maker of astrolabes [7].

The 11th century saw at least two well-educated women who travelled widely and left their mark as scholars: Fatimah bint Sa'd al-Khayr, who taught men alongside women in Damascus and Jerusalem, and Umm al-Kiram Karimah bint Ahmad ibn Muhammad ibn Hatim al-Maarwaziyyah, who was a popular storyteller, dying in Mecca at the age of 100 [8]. Another educator of both men and women was the 14th-century Fatimah al-Bataihiyyah, whose pupils assembled in the mosque of the Prophet himself in Medina [9]. And there are more. In his *al-Muhaddithat: The Women Scholars in Islam*, Carla Power's friend and mentor, Mohammad Akram Nadwi, documents nearly 9,000 Muslim women from the 7th to the 20th century who were noted scholars [10].

Today the clerics and their submissive governments in Iran and Pakistan, as well as in Saudi Arabia (where the roles are reversed), convince the people and adherents of Islam elsewhere that androcentrism is central to their religion. Yet the key paragraphs of chapter 4 ('On women') of the Qu'ran, namely Verse 4:34, contain no mention of androcentric strictures [11]. Critics of Muslim culture, though, should remember that the ten numerals (0–9) we use universally today are of Arab origin. The concept of zero had been developed in India two centuries earlier, around 500, and hints of it were evident already in pharaonic Egypt, in Babylon and in pre-Columbian Meso-America.

Joining a convent was mainly for the better-off, as it required an aspirant for admission to hand over money or land. The poor might enter if there was a menial job available. Life in a convent enabled those wishing to avoid marriage to do so. Most establishments were a kind of seminary, providing an education for all and allowing some ambitious women to achieve their potential.

Of course the difference between the lives of the rich and the poor continued to exceed that between men and women, and would do so well beyond the 20th century. Likewise the nobility, including women, enjoyed a freedom of action denied to the rest of the population. As historian

Rodney Hilton put it, 'It should not be necessary to write a separate history of half the beings in any social class. We must, however, do so, whether or not we believe that all women through history have constituted a class oppressed by all men or whether we believe that women's class position was more important than their sex' [12]. It was during the Middle Ages that women found their voice. Through the pen they gave us homilies, poems and stories. By their actions they showed an ability to lead and to confront powerful men. With their generosity they endowed many monasteries for women, as well as famous seats of learning (for men). Their intellect and drive enabled some to become acknowledged physicians.

Women's Daily Lives

The respect that women achieved during the Middle Ages is apparent already in the 4th century. St Augustine of Hippo — he of 'Lord, make me chaste, but not yet' — entered into correspondence with a number of lay women. Copies of his letters, though none from the recipients, have survived. Written in Latin, it is clear that he expected the reader to understand this language. And many did. Moreover, 'one notion consistently emerges from Augustine's letters to women, a sense of the women's authority: their authority to speak, to write, to make decisions; their authority over others, and how to use it ... Women are expected, by Augustine, at any rate, to take the initiative and make their own decisions. ... Reading the space between these letters, then, does indeed yield some clues to women's literacy and its relationship with their power and authority in the wider world' [13].

Women's lives during the Middle Ages, whether peasant or noble-woman, in rural and urban environments, from Egypt to Anglo-Saxon England, were dominated by spinning and weaving. The very words have come down to us as 'spinsters' and 'wives' [14]. Another major occupation was brewing. Prior to the introduction of hops during the 14th century to make beer, ale made from barley was the universal drink. Wealthy lords and ladies may have drunk wine, but few drank water, and for good reason. Although microbes would not be recognised until the 17th century, their malign influence on consumers of water from contaminated rivers and lakes was well appreciated. Men checked the quality of the brew, but the task of producing it fell on women [15]. Women also worked in the fields alongside men as they had done for millennia. They baked bread and washed clothes — in their own homes and in those of the nobility (where other domestic duties were carried out by men) — and took their produce to market. Although generally paid less than men for similar work, in the case of bringing in the harvest or for thatching a roof, their remuneration was the same [16].

During the middle of the 14th century, the plague that become known as the Black Death spread across Eurasia. The disease was transmitted through the bite of fleas infected with bacteria known as *Yersinia pestis* that reside in the fur of rats. Once arrived in an impoverished, unhygienic household, body lice as well as fleas continued to spread the disease without rodent support. The outcome of a bite is a painful swelling of the lymph nodes (known as buboes). The infection spreads through the body, often causing death through pneumonia. Over 30% of Europe's population succumbed to this pandemic. The peasantry were more affected than the nobility, who escaped to the seclusion of their estates. With fewer men available to carry out day-to-day tasks, over the following years women took over some of the work and were accordingly rewarded with a newly found freedom to bargain. Moreover the rights of widows, which were already considerable, were improved. But the extent to which this was indeed a favourable time for women is arguable.

Within a convent the chief occupation, of course, was prayer, reflection and joining in the services led by male clergy. Lay duties included cultivation of cereals and vegetables grown in fields attached to the monastery. In the garden within the walls, medicinal plants were grown, which the nuns dispensed to the sick. They washed clothes, cooked food, harvested honey and produced ale and wine. They were involved in spinning and weaving, in embroidery and the illumination of manuscripts. Senior nuns provided an education for novices.

Most women outside the cloister were married, and unlike the views of certain Tudors in the 16th century, infertility in marriage was not necessarily laid at the door of the wife. In the 11th century it was women, from both ends of society, who recorded the Norman Conquest of England and the events leading up to it by their beautifully embroidered pictorial record known as the Bayeux Tapestry. Remarkably the original exists and may be seen in a museum in the town of Bayeux. A meticulously reproduced version, completed in 1886, is displayed in the Reading Museum in the town of that name in England.

During the 13th century there developed in Flanders a movement for women of a spiritual nature, who were not bound by religious orthodoxy. It was known as beguine, and its participants as beguines. The idea of women living in an essentially lay community, able to develop their spirituality, caught on and spread to France, the Rhineland and beyond. Beguines were not necessarily impoverished women. Many came from a growing middle class, able to contribute to their upkeep. Several enlarged the community by building extra houses within the walls of the establishment. These were endowed not by ecclesiastical institutions, but by female sponsors such as Jeanne, Countess of Flanders, and after her death by her sister and successor, Margaret. The latter founded the beguinage in Lille, one of the largest in Europe. It included a herb garden and other amenities, and continued to function well into the 19th century [17]. The Countesses of Flanders did not restrict themselves to beguinages, but endowed also Cistercian monasteries for women in Ghent and Hainaut. Jeanne was indefatigable in her support of worthy causes, whether helping workers in the wool trade or improving navigation along the river Lys.

Much of medieval literature was composed inside a convent or beguinage. Before recounting the lives of some of these authors, I need to mention a lady who was neither a nun nor a European.

Women's Voices

She was the Japanese writer **Murasaki** (or Izumi) **Shikibu** (*c* 978–*c* 1016), and was probably the first novelist in the world. Her literary calling was fostered by an unorthodox childhood. In the Heian era, husbands and wives kept separate households and children were brought up by their mothers. Murasaki's mother died in childbirth, so she was raised by her father.

Literary Chinese (the language of learning) was considered an exclusively male preserve but Murasaki learned it by listening to her brother's tutorials. She later wrote that her father said of her: 'If only you were a boy, how happy I would be.' Unlike most Japanese women, who married at puberty, Murasaki waited until her mid-20s to marry her father's friend, a much older second cousin, whom she loved. Her husband died after the birth of her daughter which threw her into prolonged grief. As a lady in waiting at the imperial court [18] she was able to indulge in her passion for poetry and prose. This resulted in *The Diary of Lady Murasaki* and *The Tale of Genji* (one of the first writings in the Japanese language). *The Tale of Genji*, a trilogy in 54 chapters, took her over a decade to write. Emotionally intelligent and sensitive, Murasaki chronicled the fragility of life, speaking of universal concerns in a timeless voice. The loneliness of the artist inhabiting a solitary inner world informed her writing. A court lady described her prose in 1007: 'There is a fragrance even in her smallest words.' Reviewers subsequently compared *Genji* to the writings of Austen, Proust and Shakespeare.

Another woman, whose legacy is not spiritual, was **Trota of Salerno** (1050–1097). She led a community of women in Salerno devoted to the treatment of the sick. They practised surgery as well as medical interventions. They advised on cosmetics and skin diseases. The school was entirely independent of any ecclesiastical establishment. It 'gained a reputation for its scientific and practical course of study and qualified as the first European university' [19]. Trota's scientific writing includes studies on infertility and birth control. Together with two other (unidentified) authors the work of the Salerno school has recently been edited and translated (from Latin) [20]. The original work served as a 'standard medical school text until the sixteenth century' [21]. The practice of medicine by women spread to Germany where it was accepted throughout the Middle Ages. Elsewhere, however, female participation in medicine became suspect already in the 14th century. Their role was deemed unnatural and they were considered to be no more than witches. So medicine is but another freedom accorded to women during the early medieval period and subsequently removed.

Back to the cloister. The tenth child of a well-connected German family, **Hildegard von Bingen** (1098–1179) became known as the 'Sybil of the Rhine' [22]. At eight years of age her family put her under the tutelage of an acquaintance and at 14 she entered the monastery of Disibodenberg under the abbess Jutta von Sponheim. Since early childhood Hildegard suffered from ill health while experiencing intense visions of divine origin. Neurologist Oliver Sacks thought that they might have been brought on by attacks of migraine [23]. In 1136 Jutta died and Hildegard, not yet 40, was appointed to succeed her. Considering herself divinely inspired, she found the authority to speak where few women were permitted a voice. The Benedictine canon that a cloister is for life, she ignored. At the age of 61 she travelled along the Rhine to preach in churches and monasteries (specifically forbidden). She wrote innumerable letters — in Latin — to senior church figures, including the pope (one of whom was Nicholas Breakspear, the newly elected, and so far the only, English pope). Her message was simple: the clergy were forsaking humility in favour of temporal power (preceding by some 350 years Martin Luther's strictures along similar lines).

Royalty were not exempt from her missives. Frederick Barbarossa, the most powerful man in Europe, was intimidated enough to grant the newly constructed monastery at Rupertsberg, to which Hildegard had been appointed abbess, imperial protection from his troops that were ravaging the surrounding countryside. Hildegard's curiosity in matters other than ecclesiastical was unmatched. 'She was a polymath: a visionary, a theologian, a preacher; an early scientist and physician; a prodigious letter writer ... She was an artist not only in the musical and literary sense but in painting ... Her boldness, courage and tenacity made her at once enthralling and haughty, intrepid and irksome' [24]. She wrote nine botanical and medicinal texts in which she listed almost 1,000 plants and animals, examined the causes and cures of diseases, then offered remedies. 'Bladder of sturgeon soothes dropsy, liver of turbot rubbed on the eyes is recommended for clouded sight, powdered salmon bones are a remedy for rotting gums. Arnica ... was considered a potent aphrodisiac' [25]. She was devoted to music and composed 80 songs, a morality play, and accompaniments for special feast days. Contemporary composers have incorporated her chants into their own work and in Oxford a girls' choir is named after her. She is considered a saint by the church, and the most distinguished naturalist and original 12th-century philosopher in Western Europe by others [26].

In 1967 a German historian, Dieter Schaller, came across more than 100 love letters in the library of Clairvaux Abbey, situated in the champagne country of northern France. They had lain there since the end of the 15th century when a monk called Johannes de Vepria had copied them from even earlier documents. He had named the letters *Epistolae duorum amantium* (*Letters of two lovers*), which led Schaller and others to wonder whether these were the long-lost letters allegedly exchanged between **Héloise** (1090/1100–1164) and Abélard (1079–1142) during the early decades of the 12th century [27]. Héloise, reputedly the illegitimate daughter of two members of the French nobility, had been taken to live in Paris with one Fulbert, a canon of Notre Dame. He referred to her as his niece and ward, though she may equally have been his natural daughter. Héloise was a clever girl and Uncle Fulbert decided to give the teenager a good education by engaging a budding philosopher, Pierre Abélard, for this purpose. Fulbert invited the teacher to lodge at his house (though he subsequently regretted this). As you may have guessed by now, pupil and mentor fell in love. Their story has become a legend, so well-known outside France that they are generally referred to as Heloise and Peter Abelard.

Needless to say that — behind her uncle's back — Heloise became pregnant. Peter begged her to marry him, but she refused, aware of the scandal this would cause. Instead Peter arranged for her to stay in Brittany for her confinement. Having delivered herself of a son whom she called Astrolabe, she returned to Paris. She now agreed to the marriage, reluctantly attended by Fulbert, while Astrolabe disappears from historical records. The newlyweds realised they could no longer live under Fulbert's roof. Somewhat perversely Peter encouraged his wife to take the veil in a convent at Argenteuil, where she subsequently became abbess. The affair continued with frequent visits by Peter who somehow managed to consummate his love for Heloise without the other nuns' knowledge. It ended only when Fulbert's rage led him to send a servant to castrate Peter. The mission was seemingly successful. The letters between the two continued, many now in verse [28]. It has been suggested that Heloise's letters were forged by Abelard, but this has been robustly dismissed [29].

In relation to the early letters exchanged between Heloise and Abelard after their first meeting, Giles Constable, a professor at Princeton, wonders why two people living under one roof should write to each other at all. (Perhaps this is not so odd. I am aware of an elderly academic couple living together in Oxford who used to send each other notes, though admittedly they were not on speaking terms much of the time.) Constable admits that 'the letters certainly show an astonishing degree and type of learning, verging at times on pedantry, for a girl of sixteen or seventeen.' He concludes that 'those who question the attribution of the early letters "reflect an unwillingness to accept that such a gifted and independently minded woman could have existed in twelfth century France"' [30].

Of all the letters, perhaps the only truly authenticated is one by Heloise, and it isn't to Abelard. She had left Argenteuil in 1129, when the convent was taken over by the Abbey of St Denis in Paris, and relocated to the Oratory of the Paraclete, 110 km southeast of Paris. Abelard, who by now had himself become a monk and then abbott (having narrowly avoided excommunication by Pope Innocent II), died in 1142. The letter Heloise wrote was to Abelard's friend Peter the Venerable, Abbott of Cluny. In it she thanks the Abbott for having conducted a requiem Mass for Abelard and for sending her 'the body of our master' [31].

Another person whose authorship of surviving manuscripts is uncertain was **Marie de France** (*c* 1160–*c* 1215). She appears to have been born in France, but to have spent most of her life in England. I mention her only because she wrote — in early French, though it is clear that she knew Latin — very much for a lay audience. Unlike Hildegard von Bingen and others, she does not stricture the abuses of clerics. She writes to entertain, with stories about fictional people, one of which is set in the medical community of Salerno. Marie was concerned that, being a woman, some of her anecdotes would be plagiarised by men (which was not unreasonable). She is considered 'a figure of literary importance' [32] because her 'breadth of learning, her charming, subtle literary style, sagacious mind and sensitive spirit are captivating' [33].

A particularly gifted beguine was **Mechtild** (1207–1282), daughter of a Saxon nobleman. Following a series of visions in her childhood, she left the family home in her early twenties and entered a beguinage at Magdeburg in northeastern Germany. In due course she was appointed to an administrative position. This was normal. Just as an abbess was in charge of a convent, so women supervised the members of a beguinage. A monk or friar would come in to conduct divine service. Mechtild became interested in the Dominican Order, which she was able to join in a lay capacity. She now began to set down her visions, pausing to criticise church leaders in the way Hildegard von Bingen had done in the previous century, which engendered attempts to burn her work. Writing in the vernacular, she spent the next 30 years on the project. The outcome was a monumental work in seven books entitled *Das fließende Licht der Gottheid* (*The Flowing Light of Divinity*). Two events now altered her life. Her health deteriorated and she became blind. Then, at over 60 years of age, she entered the Cistercian convent at Helfta, some 80 km south of Magdeburg.

Helfta was noted for encouraging intellectual discourse among its nuns. Novices were taught the *trivium* (grammar, rhetoric and logic) and the more able the *quadrivium* (arithmetic, geometry, astronomy, music) as well. Here Mechtild met a namesake, **Mechtild of Hackeborn** (1241–1298), and one Gertrude (1256–1302; later **Gertrude the Great**). Both had entered the convent before their eighth birthday. Gertrude became abbess at 19 years of age. Through their joint writings they advanced 'a devotional cult which reflected their shared female biology and gave spiritual expression to their sense of community' [34]. At Helfta Mechtild of Magdeburg completed her opus, while Gertrude and Mechtild of Hackeborn recorded their own visions: *Legatus divinae pietatis* (*The Herald of God's Loving-Kindness*) by Gertrude and *Liber specialis gratiae* (*The Book of Special Grace*) by Mechtild. All three nuns followed the concept of the Sacred Heart. If a sense of femininity epitomises the Middle Ages, it finds its utmost expression in the vision of the Sacred Heart. This is 'a site of female biological characteristics: it bleeds, it flows, it opens, it encloses. Sometimes it is most overwhelmingly fleshly. Medieval illustrations of the Sacred Heart resemble nothing so much as a vagina. The wound was graphically represented as a slit between two gaping edges; sometimes, but not always, drops of blood were shown emerging' [35]. These three visionaries 'rewrote their culture by inscribing the female on the divine'. They developed 'a devotional cult which reflected their shared female biology and gave spiritual expression to their sense of community' [36].

The beguine movement developed also in southern Europe. In the town of Digne in Provence was born a girl called **Douceline** (1214–1274), daughter of a wealthy merchant. Her upbringing was along strictly religious lines and at 20 years of age a vision led her to renounce her current life. She took a vow of chastity and pious devotion in front of her brother Hugh, a Franciscan monk. Aware of the beguine movement in the north she founded her own beguinage in Hyères on the Mediterranean coast, 200 km south of her birthplace. This proved so successful with her charges — many of whom were well-educated women — that she was able to establish another beguinage outside Marseilles. Douceline has been described as 'a powerful woman, able to out-preach and out-perform every cleric present' [37].

To Scandinavia, where the daughter of a rich land-owning knight living in Uppland on the east coast of Sweden, just north of Stockholm, became one of six patron saints of Europe. She was named Birgitta (Bridget) and has come down to us as **Birgitta of Sweden** (1303–1373). At the age of 14 she married a well-born man with whom she had eight children: six survived into maturity. Birgitta was a devout person, full of good works, and together with husband Ulf went on a pilgrimage to Santiago de Compostela. Unfortunately Ulf died shortly afterwards and Birgitta joined the Third Order of St Francis which encompasses men and women, religious and lay. She now decided to found her own movement, generally referred to as the Birgittines. Katherine Zieman, an expert in late medieval literature, sums up Birgitte's contribution — especially in relation to the opening paragraph of this chapter — as follows. 'It was in the field of liturgy that Birgitta of Sweden made some of her more radical gestures towards reenvisioning women's relation to both clerical knowledge and ecclesiastical authority. Foremost of these gestures, of course, was the very creation and institution of a distinctive Bridgittine rite. A unique version of the Office of the Virgin performed by the women of the double monastic community, the Bridgittine Office provided a text of divine origin that validated the women's community in particular. The service itself, and especially the lessons of the *Sermo angelicus*', composed by Birgitta, 'read daily at matins, went further to articulate a powerful Mariology that ... was meant to instruct the Bridgittine community to reflect the exemplary authority it granted to the Virgin Mary in the early Christian community' [38].

Some pious medieval women chose to live in total seclusion. One such was **Julian of Norwich** (1343–sometime after 1416), more accurately described as Juliana. Her actual name and origins are unknown and the name Julian derives solely from the fact that she spent most of her life as an anchoress in a cell attached to the church of St Julian in Norwich. (This was hit during an air raid in 1942 and has been rebuilt as a shrine to her memory.) Before entering her cell, Julian may have mothered a child who died during the Black Death that took half the population of Norwich with it. As an anchoress, she would be incarcerated in her cell for life. She would have received her food and missives through an opening onto the street. When this was covered by a curtain she could converse through it with visitors. Her participation in the Mass was through a window into the adjacent church. Throughout her life Julian experienced divine visions, particularly of Jesus, which she recorded as *Revelations of Divine Love*, a manuscript that happily for us has been preserved and is now in the British Museum. Probably the least educated of the women I have mentioned, Julian wrote not in Latin but in the vernacular. *Revelations of Divine Love* is therefore considered to be the earliest book in English (a fusion of Saxon and Old French by the 14th century) to be written by a woman. Her writings have been described as 'always novel, never new' by some [39], 'earthshaking' by others [40].

Christine de Pizan (1364–1430) was born of a professional father whose family came from Pizzano, southeast of Bologna. From the age of four she lived in Paris. At 15 she married and bore three children, after which her husband died of the plague. Through the patronage of members of the French court Christine was able to support her family by writing a number of influential works as well as poetry. She had read Boccaccio's *De mulieribus* (*Of women*) in which he writes that women's *ingenium* (genius, imagination, intellect, intelligence, mind, talent, wisdom) is shown by their invention of, or skill in, 'the plow, the Egyptian alphabet, cultivation of flax and hemp, weaving, prophetic writing, the Latin language, divination by fire, the battle-ax, cotton combing, new poetic forms, philosophical critique, poetic composition, Heliconoan verse and the cento' [41]. Christine condenses Boccaccio's rambling by remarking that many inventions 'have been discovered through women's creative intelligence and subtlety'. Intriguingly she wonders whether 'as a compensation for relatively slighter physique women may display a beneficial mental agility: they have minds more *delivre* (liberated, freed) or more nimble than men's when they apply themselves' [42].

Margery Kempe (1373–1438) was born in Bishop's Lynn (now King's Lynn) in Norfolk, where her father several times served as mayor of the town. At 20 she married one John Kempe with whom she went on to have 14 children. She worked in the town of her birth in the brewing business, then in milling. 'Failing spectacularly in these endeavours, she feels chastened by God, and is eventually converted to a passionately devout life' [43]. But she does not enter any religious establishment. Instead she travels to the Holy Land and to Rome, leaving behind her 14 children and husband John. She takes a vow of chastity and considers herself now to be the 'bride of Christ', on whose command she dresses in white. This proved an unfortunate decision as 'whiteness had become associated in the popular mind not with purity but with its opposite: disruption to social order and a threat to the norms of gender' [44].

Indeed, returning from a subsequent pilgrimage to Santiago de Compostela, she was apprehended and 'questioned, abused, once threatened with rape, repeatedly threatened with burning, denounced from pulpits, and publicly examined on four separate occasions on suspicion of heresy, insurrection, unlawful preaching, and leading women astray' [45]. Each time, Kempe was eventually acquitted. Like Trota of Salerno,

Heloise, and Marie de France, Margery Kempe cannot be unequivocally associated with her writings. *The Book of Margery Kempe* came to the notice of literary scholars only in 1934 and debate about its exact authorship endures. The *Book* is largely an account of Margery Kempe's life. Like Julian of Norwich whom she visited, Margery Kempe was no Latin scholar. So the *Book* is written in the vernacular, which makes it 'the earliest extant autobiographical work in English' [46].

Women of Action

Four women are particularly worthy of mention. The first is **Aethelflaed** (*c* 870–918), eldest daughter of Alfred the Great. Her origins are therefore in Wessex, which covered much of southwest England. But she married one Aethelred, Lord of Mercia (that then extended over today's Gloucestershire, Worcestershire, Herefordshire and Shropshire) and so moved north. At her husband's death she became 'Lady of Mercia' and thus the only female ruler of a kingdom in Anglo-Saxon England. This resolute lady built fortifications to defend her territory and as a result was able to see off several invasions by Vikings from Brittany. Apart from Wessex and Mercia, the rest of England was then occupied by the Danes. Aethelflaed's army now took Leicester off her foreign neighbour. Seeing which way the wind was blowing, York decided to switch sides to Mercian rule. It was from such military successes that Aethelflaed's 'fame spread abroad in every direction' [47].

Eleanor of Aquitaine (1122–1204) is considered to be 'the twelfth century's most famous woman' [48]. Her father, Duke of Aquitaine and of Gascony and Count of Poitou, gave her an excellent education and, on his death, a huge inheritance. As Duchess of Aquitaine, which she governed in her own right, she was the most eligible bride in France. Not surprisingly she married the king, Louis VII. She continued her patronage of troubadours and artists, while bearing her husband two daughters. When the king set off on the Second Crusade, Eleanor was at his side. But her royal consort began to bore her and she sought an annulment (on the grounds of failing to produce an heir). She managed to persuade the Church and the marriage was duly annulled. Eleanor was determined that her wealth be put to good use. If not to France, then why not to her old enemy England? Eleanor and Henry Plantagenet had met a year earlier and the encounter proved fruitful. They married in 1152, the groom 19 years of age, the bride 30. It was, for a while, a successful marriage. At Henry's coronation in 1154 as Henry II by the Archbishop of Canterbury, Eleanor was crowned Queen. Over the following years Eleanor produced eight children for Henry: five sons, two of whom would become kings of England (Richard I the Lionheart, and John).

Relations cooled sharply when Eleanor supported their eldest son in rebelling against his father. Henry responded by imprisoning her, or at least restricting her movements. Eleanor continued to support her children, and to exercise her own authority, especially after Henry's death in 1189. Thus when her favourite son, now Richard I, was captured while returning from his crusade, Eleanor was in part *de facto* ruler of England. On Richard's release she effected a reconciliation between him and his ambitious brother John, and at the age of 72 she retired to the abbey of Fontevrault in northwest France. But she was not done yet. Six years later she journeyed across the Pyrenees (in winter) to support her daughter, Queen Eleanor of Castile, who was arranging a marriage for her own daughter Blanche. A contemporary chronicler, Richard of Devizes, a typically misogynist monk of Winchester Cathedral, had to admit that she was 'an incomparable woman, beautiful yet virtuous, powerful yet gentle, humble yet keen-witted, qualities which are most rarely found in a woman, who had two kings as husbands and two kings as sons, still tireless in all labours at whose ability her age might marvel' [49]. According to Canadian historian Margaret Wade Labarge, 'the best known of all medieval queens is undoubtedly Eleanor of Aquitaine' [50].

Tamar of Georgia (*c* 1160–1213) is a relatively unknown figure to most readers of this book. To others 'she is considered one of the greatest of medieval Georgia's monarchs, and she presided over its greatest territorial expansion ...' [51] during what has been called the country's Golden Age. Her father, King George III, made her his heir and co-ruler in 1178. When he died six years later, Tamar overcame strong opposition from both clergy and nobility in order to be acclaimed as queen in her own right. She acquiesced to the council of nobles' choice of husband but managed to divorce him when his drunken behaviour (and alleged homosexuality) became too much for her. Instead she married a man of her own choice, prince David Soslan. He proved worthy of her choice. Leading Tamar's army against Georgia's powerful neighbour, the Seljuk Sultanate, he won several battles and extended Georgia's influence as far west as Erzurum. The enraged Sultan Rukn ad-Din Süleyman Shah informed Tamar that he would make her his wife if she converted to Islam. If not, he would make her his concubine. Tamar responded by winning yet another battle against the Sultan's army. She had by now extended Georgia's boundaries further than it would ever achieve again.

In contrast few readers will not have heard of **Joan of Arc** (*c* 1412–1431). She was born to a peasant family in the village of Domrémy, situated in the uplands of the Vosges. Her mother is responsible for teaching her to pray, and for not bothering her with much of an education. Her knowledge of contemporary history she learnt from the Saints Margaret and Katherine, who appeared to her in visions when she was barely a teenager. They told her that she would lead France to victory against the English and thus end the conflict that had been going on for nigh on 100 years. In order to fulfil this spiritual destiny Joan felt that it would be appropriate to wear male clothes and to inform Charles the Dauphin, who was prosecuting the war on behalf of the king, of his new divinely appointed commander. Charles had been told that this extraordinary young lady was on her way across France to meet him at his court in Chinon in northwest France. In order to test her apparent ability to foresee events and to recognise people she had never met, he hid himself among the crowd of courtiers. Joan immediately picked him out and introduced herself. Charles was intrigued and asked Jean Gerson, Chancellor of the University of Paris and a noted ecclesiastical scholar, to test Joan's assertion that she was sent by God to lead France to victory. Gerson accepted her claims, and Charles agreed that she might ride with the army.

Not only that, but this young (she was barely 18 years old) female in man's attire inspired the dispirited French army to renewed vigour. The English, who had besieged the town of Orleans for more than six months, were sent on their way. Further military successes followed with Joan — though wounded by an arrow — as good as leading the army. The French now had their sights on relieving Paris itself. But Joan would not be present. After a year in battle she was captured at Compiègne (where World War I would end 500 years later) and sold to the Burgundians, who were allied with the English against the French crown. Accused of heresy, she was put on trial. This was conducted by the Bishop of Rouen, whose sympathies lay with the English. The saviour of France sent by God had become a witch sent by Satan. Four months later she was found guilty of heresy and burned at the stake in the old market in Rouen. But her achievements could not be denied. Thibault d'Armagnac, who had fought on behalf of the Dauphin in Orleans, where he met Joan, thought that 'she behaved like the most experienced captain in all the world, one who had been educated in warfare for an entire lifetime.' The Duke of Alençon considered Joan to have 'held herself magnificently … especially in the setting up of artillery' [52]. Winston Churchill regarded her as 'the winner in the whole of French history'. In relation to this entire chapter, I note that he went on to say that 'the leading women of those days were more remarkable and forceful than the men' [53].

Women of Patronage

I mentioned the beneficence of the Countesses of Flanders. The medieval world saw several examples by women of independent minds and means. I will mention just three who were involved in the foundation of four Oxbridge colleges (all of course male at this time).

Elisabeth de Burgh, Lady of Clare (1295–1360), a granddaughter of Edward I, was heiress to her father Gilbert de Clare's great wealth. This was increased by marriage (at 13) to John de Burgh, heir to the earldom of Ulster. He died five years later and Elizabeth married Theobald de Verbon, who lasted no more than a few months. Next came Roger Damory, with whom she had nine years of somewhat boisterous marriage. By the age of 27 she was a thrice-widowed mother with three children. Worse, she was now imprisoned — together with her son from John de Burgh — by her powerful brother-in-law with whom Roger Damory had quarrelled, in Barking Abbey. It would be another five years before her life improved and she could settle in her father's Castle of Clare in Suffolk. She recovered the lands that had been taken from her, and now owned property in East Anglia, Dorset, Wales and Ireland. She had half her life still to live, and she spent it in support of worthy causes.

Elizabeth based herself in Clare Castle, living quietly on her own (apart from seven ladies of the chamber, each with her own maidservant, and a household of 250 other servants). The accounts show her distributing alms to more than 5,000 people over a typical five-month period. She supported Augustinian friars and Franciscan nuns: the former by building them dormitory, refectory and chapter-house on her land, the latter by inviting them to stay at her London residence. The second oldest college in Cambridge, founded in 1326, was named Clare Hall (later just Clare) when Elizabeth endowed it a decade later. She continued her benefactions for the rest of her life. In her last year she set out statutes by which the college was to be governed. Her 'remarkably enlightened attitude to learning and university education in these statutes has guided the college for nearly seven centuries' [54].

Another aristocratic lady was **Philippa of Hainault** (1310/1315–1369). She married the reforming English king Edward III, whom she served well by bearing him 12 children. The eldest was Edward of Woodstock (his birthplace), also known as the Black Prince (probably on account of the colour of his armour). Queen Philippa was a lady of good intentions. She managed to dissuade her husband from massacring the Burghers of Calais after his victory over the town. She enlarged the royal gardens (as well as her extensive wardrobe, which she could ill afford). Her chaplain Robert de Eglesfield thought so highly of her that he named the Oxford centre of learning founded by him in 1341 after her: the Queen's College.

Margaret Beaufort (1441/1443–1509), too, was born into the nobility. Her father John was Duke of Somerset and a grandson of John of Gaunt (born in Ghent, hence his name). Her mother Margaret Beauchamp was the daughter of Sir John Beauchamp of Bletsoe. Margaret Beaufort was herself a great-granddaughter of Gaunt, which would give her son the lineage required to succeed Richard III as King Henry VII. But it is remarkable that Henry was ever born at all. Margaret was just six years old when her parents decided that she should become betrothed to one John de la Pole. Three years later the parents realised that they had made a mistake and were able to replace Margaret's spouse with Edmund Tudor, son of Welshman Owen Tudor and dowager queen Catherine de Valois. Edmund was then in his early 20s. As indicated above, the year of Margaret's birth is in doubt (though the day, 31 May, is not). Many historians favour 1443, which means that Henry, who was born on 28 January 1457, was conceived before his mother's 13th birthday. Edmund died of the plague six months later. His child widow had not been put off by her early confinement and within three years she had agreed to marry Sir Henry Stafford. Their marriage was a success and lasted until Stafford's death in 1471. Within months Margaret married Thomas Stanley, Earl of Darby, whom she outlived by five years. But she never had another child.

Throughout her adult life Margaret's first concern was for her son. Remember that the Wars of the Roses were raging at this time and the life of a potential king was always in danger. Fortunately her third father-in-law, the powerful Duke of Buckingham, helped to protect young Henry. Even after Henry's accession to the throne in 1485, Margaret continued to support him. He responded by allotting her 'a share in most of his public and private resources' [55]. Yet her son was not the only recipient of her goodness. According to her contemporary Bishop Fisher, she was forever 'giving alms to the poor and needy, and dressing them also when they were sick and ministering unto them meat and drink' [56]. Although her marriage to Stanley was happy enough, in her mid-50s she took a vow of chastity (like Margery Kempe) and moved to set up her own establishment at Collyweston in Northamptonshire, where Stanley was a frequent visitor. She immersed herself in judicial tasks, building projects and managing the estate. Her legacy, however, lies elsewhere.

In 1437 William Byngham established a centre of learning in Cambridge, on a site now occupied by King's College Chapel, which he called God's House. Four years later King's College, a much larger foundation, had its eye on this riverside site. God's House, with a new royal charter, moved to the centre of the town in 1448 and changed its name to Christ's. But it now needed a much larger endowment. The Lady Margaret Beaufort was consulted and agreed to fund, and indeed to expand, the college which finally opened in 1505. It had been John Fisher, Bishop of Rochester and Margaret's chaplain, who had had the idea of turning St John's Hospital in Cambridge into a scholastic establishment. Margaret was impressed by his enthusiasm and agreed to endow the college. Although this was not formally established until 1511, two years after her death, it would not have happened without Margaret's generosity. Yet it would take almost 400 years before Margaret's name would be linked directly to that of an Oxbridge college. In 1878 Oxford University agreed to found a college specifically for the education of women. It was called Lady Margaret Hall. Bernard André, a 15th-century Augustinian friar and scholar, defined Margaret Beaufort's character, especially in relation to the gist of this book, as well as anyone when he described her as being 'steadfast and more stable than the weakness in women suggests' [57].

Medieval women had already lost status during the 11th century. 'Whereas Anglo-Saxon women could make wills and hold land, and therefore bequeath chattels and property to whomever they chose, Anglo-Norman women could do neither' [58]. The Reformation made things worse. Martin Luther may have encouraged women 'to turn away and leave the convent' [59] but he really didn't need to. The dissolution of the monasteries, especially in Tudor England, restricted the opportunities that had opened up for women during the medieval period.

This chapter began with the proposition that one of the factors favouring women during the Middle Ages was the rise of Christianity. In particular, the concept of the feminine as the human side of God. I will end with reference to one woman, a 'most Catholic queen', who was able to suppress her innate empathy by persecuting to the death those who failed to adopt her religion. She was Isabella of Castile, and her reign (she died in 1504) has been considered by some historians to mark the end of the Medieval Period.

Androcentrism was ignored by Isabella: if any female was determined to be her own woman it was Isabella I. When her half-brother Henry IV of Castile died, she had herself crowned queen in Segovia within an hour of his funeral mass. Neither Isabella's husband Ferdinand nor Henry's desired successor, his 13-year-old daughter Juana, had time to reach Segovia. In fact Isabella had made sure that her proclamation as queen of Castile was made in the absence of Ferdinand (who was supposed to be co-regent with her of Aragon and Castile). In later years, in letters ostensibly from the two co-regents, she would sign herself boldly as '*Yo, la Reyna*' [60].

Notes

1. from *c* 500–*c* 1500 CE, or the fall of Rome to the Protestant Reformation. Others consider the ending to be represented by the fall of Constantinople (1453), by Columbus's first voyage of discovery (1492), or by the reconquest of Granada in the same year.
2. Bynum (1984).
3. the monastery atop Monte Cassino was virtually obliterated during World War II. But not for the first time. The buildings had been burnt down by the Saracens in 884, then rebuilt, then sacked again by Napoleon in 1799. The monastery was rebuilt after the war and reconsecrated in 1964.
4. Jane Tibbetts Schulenburg: Women's monastic communities, 500–1100: Patterns of expansion and decline. *Signs* **14**: 261–292 (1989).
5. taken from Mohammad Akram Nadwi: *al-Muhaddithat: The Women Scholars in Islam* (London: Interface, 2007) and quoted in Power (2015), p 28.
6. from 1001 Inventions: https://www.1001inventions.com/feature/womens-day/
7. *ibid*.
8. taken from Mohammad Akram Nadwi: *al-Muhaddithat: The Women Scholars in Islam* (London: Interface, 2007) and quoted in Power (2015), pp 130 and 131.
9. *ibid*, p 129.
10. mentioned by Power (2015), p 130.
11. Carla Power: What the Koran really says about women, *Daily Telegraph* (6 November, 2015).

12. Rodney H Hilton: *The English Peasantry in the Later Middle Ages* (Oxford: Clarendon Press, 1972), p 95; quoted by Labarge (1986), p v.

13. Catherine Conybeare: *Augustine's Correspondence with Women*; in Olson and Kerby-Fulton (2005), pp 62, 65 and 66.

14. Leyser (1996), p 14.

15. *ibid*, p 146.

16. *ibid*, p 150.

17. Penelope Galloway: *Discreet and Devout Maidens: Women's Involvement in Beguine Communities in Northern France, 1200–1500*; in Diane Watt (ed) (1997), p 99.

18. Sarashina *et al*: *Diaries of Court Ladies of Old Japan* (translated by Annie Shepley Omori and Kochi Doi, with an Introduction by Amy Lowell; Tokyo: Kenkyusha Co, 1935).

19. Alic (1986), p 50.

20. Monica H Green: *The Trotula: A Medieval Compendium of Women's Medicine* (Pennsylvania: University of Pennsylvania Press, 2020).

21. Alic (1986), p 53.

22. *ibid*, p 62.

23. Maddocks (2001), p 63.

24. *ibid*, p xi.

25. *ibid*, p 150 *et seq*.

26. Alic (1986), p 74.

27. C Stephen Jaeger: Epistolae duorum amantium *and the Ascription to Heloise and Abelard*, in Olson and Kerby-Fulton (2005), p 125.

28. taken from Project Gutenberg's Letters of Abelard and Heloise by Pierre Bayle, translated by John Hughes, and released as an ebook in 2011, which also contains eight of the letters in full.

29. Barbara Newman: Authority, authenticity and the repression of Heloise. *Journal of Medieval and Renaissance Studies* 22: 121–157 (1992).

30. Giles Constable: *The Authorship of the* Epistolae duorum amantium, in Olson and Kerby-Fulton (2005), p 167 *et seq*; the quotation is from Constant J Mews: *The lost love letters of Heloise and Abelard: Perceptions of dialogue in twelfth century France* (Basingstoke: Macmillan, 1999), p 170.

31. Christopher Baswell: *Heloise*, in Dinshaw and Wallace (2003), p 162.

32. Labarge (1986), p 234.

33. Mickel (1974), p 23; quoted by Labarge (1986), p 234.

34. Rosalynn Voaden: *All Girls Together: Community, Gender and Vision at Helfta*, in Diane Watt (1997), p 86.

35. *ibid*, p 74.

36. *ibid*, p 86.

37. Kathryn Kerby-Fulton: *When Women Preached: An Introduction to Female Homiletic, Sacramental, and Liturgical Roles in the Later Middle Ages*, in Olson and Kerby-Fulton (2005), p 44.

38. Katherine Zieman: *Playing* Doctor*: St Birgitta, Ritual Reading and Ecclesiastical Authority*, in Olson and Kerby-Fulton (2005), p 308.

39. Thomas Andrew Bennett: Julian of Norwich, the Bible, and creative, orthodox theology. *Scottish Journal of Theology* **69**: 309-325 (2016).

40. Kathryn Kerby-Fulton: *When Women Preached*, in Olson and Kerby-Fulton (2005), p 34.

41. Alcuin Blamires: *Women and Creative Intelligence in Medieval Thought*, in Olson and Kerby-Fulton (2005), p 216.

42. *ibid*, p 221.

43. Carolyn Dinshaw: *Margery Kempe*, in Dinshaw and Wallace (2003), p 223.

44. Janet Wilson: *Communities of Dissent: The Secular and Ecclesiastical Communities of Margery Kempe's* Book, in Watt (1997), p 172.

45. Nicholas Watson: *The Making of* The Book of Margery Kempe, in Olson and Kerby-Fulton (2005), p 395.

46. Carolyn Dinshaw: *Margery Kempe*, in Dinshaw and Wallace (2003), p 222.

47. quoted by Leyser (1996), p 61.

48. Ralph V Turner: Eleanor of Aquitaine, twelfth-century English chroniclers and her 'black legend'. *Nottingham Medieval Studies* **52**: 17–42 (2008).

49. quoted by Ralph V Turner, *ibid*.

50. Labarge (1986), p 50.

51. https://www.ancient.eu/Queen_Tamar/

52. both quoted by Olson and Kerby-Fulton (2005), p 234.

53. quoted in Roberts (2019), p 444.

54. from Clare College, Cambridge: College History; see http://www.clare.cam.ac.uk/College-History/

55. quoted by Jones and Underwood (1992), p 4.

56. *ibid*, p 179; quoted by Leyser (1996), p 237.

57. quoted by Jones and Underwood (1992), p 1.
58. Leyser (1996), p 74.
59. Helga Robinson-Hammerstein: *Women's Prospects in Early Sixteenth Century Germany. Did Martin Luther's Teaching Make a difference?*, in Meek and Lawless (2005), p 118.
60. Downey (2014), p 310.

Chapter 6

Resumption: Enlightenment and Hypocrisy

This chapter will deal with the attitudes towards women and their response between 1500 and 1900. The period saw more change in the world than in any previous 400 years. The continent of America was discovered by Europeans and its inhabitants deprived of their lands, their wealth and their freedom. Wars raged across Europe, including a civil one in England that led to regicide. Scientists and philosophers brought the Age of Reason, also known as the Enlightenment, to Europe. Revolutions broke out in America and in France. In 1500 the world's population was between 400 and 500 million, with a growth rate over the preceding century of less than 0.12%; by 1900 the population had increased to between 1.5 and 1.7 billion, with a growth rate over the preceding century of 0.5–0.6% [1]. Advances in medicine began to have a modest effect. Life expectancy grew from less than 35 years to around 40 years in Europe, Asia and North America (it would not reach 70 years until the end of the 20th century, and has barely reached 60 years in Africa today) [2]. In 1500 half of all infants died during their first year. By 1900 that figure had dropped to a quarter [3].

In 1558 the Scottish ecclesiastic and reformer John Knox published *The First Blast of the Trumpet against the Monstrous Regiment of Women*. His main target was Mary of Guise, widow of the Scottish king James V and regent for their six-day old daughter, Mary Queen of Scots. His ire later expanded to include Mary herself, as well as her cousins, the deceased English Queen Mary and her reigning half-sister Elizabeth. Rule by a female he considered to be unnatural and against God's will. His contemporary

John Calvin, whom Knox met in Geneva, took a different view and urged his friend against publication, but Knox went even further. All women were inferior to men, capable only of bearing children: serving men was their godly duty. Knox's views were by no means atypical of his time, which is why I have titled this chapter Resumption (of androcentrism).

European Ruling Queens

The previous chapter ended with Isabella I, co-regnant Queen in Spain. She was succeeded by her daughter Joanna (the Mad) who finished up in a nunnery. Only one other regnant queen followed them: Isabella II (1830–1904), whose troubled reign from 1833 (under a regency until 1843) was ended by revolution in 1868. But elsewhere in Europe, several queens — some equally unfortunate, others not at all — emerged or forced their way to the top. I have already mentioned the impetuous and foolish Mary Queen of Scots. Her English relative Mary I (1516–1558) has come to be known as Bloody Mary on account of her determined persecution (probably egged on by her Spanish husband Philip) of Protestants who had risen to prominence during the reign of her half-brother Edward VI. Mary I's return of England to Catholicism was reversed when her half-sister Elizabeth (see below) became queen. Three more regnant queens, Mary II (1662–1694, co-ruler with husband William III), Anne (1665–1714) and Victoria (1819–1901) followed.

In Poland, the Jagiellonian Anne (1523–1586) was appointed co-regent with Stephen Báthory in 1575 (following the elected king's departure on becoming Henri III of France). In Sweden, Christina (1626–1689) ruled from the age of 18 until her abdication in 1654. In Russia, Catherine I (1684–1727) ruled for two years after the death of her husband, Peter I, in 1725. Within less than 40 years, three further women would become queens regnant in Russia: Anne (1693–1740), Elizabeth (1709–1762) and Catherine II (see below). In Austria, Maria Theresa (see below) reigned over the Hapsburg lands for four decades. In Portugal, Mary I (1734–1816) was known as 'the Pious'; in Brazil, over which she ruled as their first queen, she was called 'the Mad'. The roles were reversed when Mary II

(1819–1853), born in Rio de Janeiro, was proclaimed Queen of Portugal at the age of 15. The list is by no means exhaustive, but it shows that between 1500 and 1900 it was not so unusual for a woman to ascend the throne of a European country. Four ladies were so determined and shrewd that they deserve a fuller mention.

France has never had a regnant queen: Salic law prevents this. But the Florentine **Catherine de Medici** (1519–1589), daughter of Lorenzo II de Medici, came close. An orphan within a month of her birth, her life became threatened before her ninth birthday. To escape the anti-Medici mob who had taken over the city, her aunt placed her in a number of convents over the next three years. In the first she was miserable, the second was filthy and disease-ridden, but the convent of Santa-Maria Annunziata delle Murate provided a safe and friendly haven (her godmother was abbess).

The most propitious moment in Catherine's life came during the following year. Her great-uncle, Pope Clement VII, brokered (and paid for) Catherine's marriage to Henry of Orléans, second son of Francis I, king of France. 'The greatest match in the world' [4] took place in Marseilles on 28 October 1533. Bride and groom were each 14. Catherine's arrival in Paris was received with rapture. A year later her stock among the royal entourage fell sharply: Clement VII died, with part of the dowry and other promises to Francis I unfulfilled. 11 years later Catherine gave birth to a son (Francis) and over the next 12 years she would present Henry with nine more offspring, three of them boys. But apart from her seventh child Marguerite (also known as Margot) who lived to 70 years of age, the others were infirm, with three dying in infancy. In 1547 Francis I died. His son, now Henry II, asked Catherine to act as regent during the times when he was leading the French army in skirmishes against the Spanish under their ruler Philip II [5]. Catherine made impassionate speeches to the citizens of Paris, asking for men and money. She was rewarded with both. Henry's army defeated the invader and for good measure liberated Calais from the English. The following year Philip II proposed a peace treaty.

This was signed on 30 June 1559 and marked by celebrations at the Château des Tournelles in Paris. Catherine was happy that the treaty included the wedding of her eldest daughter, the 14-year-old Elizabeth, to the recently widowed 32-year-old Philip II (who deigned not to attend in person). The festivities included jousting, at which Henry challenged all comers. He successfully saw off two contenders, but a third, Gabriel, Count de Montgomery, almost knocked him off his horse. Montgomery asked leave to retire, but Henry insisted that they should continue. As Montgomery charged, a long splinter of wood from his jousting lance pierced Henry's eye: when lifted off his horse his face was in a pool of blood and his visor found half-open. He died ten days later.

The French crown now passed to Catherine's first-born, the sickly 15-year-old Francis II. The previous year Francis had been married to Mary, Queen of Scots, his senior by one year [6]. Catherine now faced three challenges: the ill health of the king and his two brothers, the growing tension between Protestants and Catholics, and the country's financial woes. Francis II died, not unexpectedly, after a reign of just 16 months. Catherine's second son, the ten-year-old Charles-Maximilien, would become King Charles IX at the official age of 15. In the meantime Catherine wrested sole regency over other contenders. As virtual ruler of France she concentrated on easing the religious conflict that was tearing the country apart. Her intentions were correct, her later methods disastrous. Catholics controlled much of the north including Paris, the Huguenots [7] the south with their main base at La Rochelle. The first war of religion left at least 3,000 Frenchmen, mainly Huguenots, dead. In 1563 the Queen Mother brokered the Edict of Amboise in order to stop the conflict. Neither side took much notice.

Charles was not even 14, but Catherine managed to have him accepted as king. He responded by asking his mother to continue her wise rule in his name. She responded by taking him on a grand tour of his realm: he would become acquainted with his possessions, and his subjects would have the opportunity to greet their new monarch. The royal progress lasted more than two years, with most of the time spent at balls and lavish entertainments in major cities between Paris and the Spanish border. To pay for this extravagance Catherine borrowed money from her Italian friends, the Strozzi bankers. It achieved little: the people continued in hunger. The religious wars, each with its own 'peace', continued. By the summer of 1572

Catherine realised that drastic action was needed to stop this folly. She now decided that a union between her daughter Marguerite and Henri King of Navarre, a Bourbon Prince of the Blood though a Huguenot, would be good for the country. There was only one snag. Because bride and groom were related — each was the great-grandchild of Charles of Angoulême — a dispensation from the pope was required. Catherine produced a forged letter to achieve this.

The Queen Mother now came to the conclusion that only the removal of the charismatic Huguenot leader, Gaspard de Coligny, would bring the religious wars to an end. In conjunction with her favourite son the king's brother Henri, Duke of Anjou, and a few selected nobles — but without informing the king — she hired an assassin. In August Coligny would be in Paris for the wedding between his protégé Henri of Navarre and Marguerite. The assassin shot Coligny in the back but missed the vital organs. With the victim alive and looked after by an enraged coterie of his friends, Catherine decided that the only way now out was to eliminate all senior Huguenots (except Princes of the Blood) gathered in Paris. This was achieved by five o'clock in the morning of Sunday 24 August, the feast day of St Bartholomew. Over the next three days the Parisian mob followed up by killing all Huguenots in Paris. The murders spread to the provinces. Within a month Catherine's plan to defuse the situation resulted in the death of an estimated loss of 20,000–30,000 innocent French lives. When she confessed her role to Charles, the king backed her up by declaring that the executions had been ordered by him. Whether people believed him is beside the point. His health deteriorated and he died, most likely of tuberculosis, less than two years later.

Over the next decade Catherine's own health began to decline. She died in agony of pleurisy on 5 January 1589. Her biographer Leonie Frieda sums her up by noting that 'she could be feminine and strangely attractive though she worked, rode, hunted and faced mortal danger with the courage of a man. … Her courage was extraordinary, her wiliness and cunning legendary' [8]. Philip II called her *La Serpente*, while a contemporary thought that 'she hath too much wit for a woman, and too little honesty for a queen' [9].

To lose one's mother at the age of three, and then one's father ten years later, is a traumatic event. But then to find oneself in the same prison in which one's mother was beheaded, and with the same possibility in view, requires exceptional fortitude to survive and to build a life. Fortunately **Elizabeth I of England** (1533–1603), like Catherine de Medici, had the character to do just that and more. Elizabeth became the most successful monarch ever to sit on the English throne [10]. Elizabeth received an education to fit her intellect. She was fluent in Latin, French and Italian, and able to converse in Greek which she read seamlessly. She was proficient in philosophy which, after music, was her favourite pastime. As Sir Robert Cecil, her Secretary of State from 1596 would remark, 'I swear by the living God her Majesty made one of the best answers extempore in Latin that ever I heard' [11]. But intellectual prowess is not sufficient in a ruler. Able leadership is the other prerequisite. Elizabeth understood this, and was able to exercise it appropriately. Having spent two months in the Tower of London at her sister Mary I's behest, Elizabeth was released and sent to live under virtual house arrest in a residence within the royal hunting park at Woodstock in Oxfordshire.

Four problems faced Elizabeth when she succeeded Mary as queen in 1558: marriage without losing control (which her sister Mary had failed to achieve), the religious state of the country after the see-sawing between Protestantism and Catholicism, the erratic behaviour of her cousin Mary Queen of Scots, and the threat from Catholic Spain. At the age of 27, and two years into her reign, Elizabeth met Robert Dudley, son of the Earl of Warwick. She was intrigued by this handsome young man and marriage plans were drawn up. But she then changed her mind, and ripped them up. Perhaps the alleged remark of Catherine de Medici that 'the queen of England is to marry her whoremaster' [12] came to her notice. The main reason Elizabeth's advisors and her parliament were keen on marriage, of course, was to secure an heir in order to achieve a smooth succession at her death. But it was not to be. The Hapsburg Archduke Charles was swiftly rejected. He was followed by Henri, Duke of Anjou, brother of the French king Charles IX. The difference in their ages (his 19 to her 37) was not the main problem: she loathed him on sight. Gradually the country came to accept Elizabeth as their Virgin Queen.

Elizabeth was careful to steer a middle course through the religious differences that were dividing the country. Practicing Catholic families were not persecuted and zealous Protestant reformers kept in check. Those who would not sign the oath of (Anglican) supremacy might not hold high office, but their lives were not in danger. When Reginald Pole, the Catholic-sympathising archbishop of Canterbury, conveniently died, he was replaced by the Protestant Matthew Parker. But the latter was not appointed to the Privy Council. So England gradually drifted back to Protestantism, where she has remained to this day.

Relations with her Scottish cousin were not so easily resolved. Mary was implicated in the murder of her former husband Henry Darnley and forced to abdicate. She then renounced her abdication and fled to England, expecting Elizabeth to restore her to the Scottish throne by force. Elizabeth made it clear that if the charges against Mary were confirmed, she should return and face justice. If found innocent, she would be free to return anyway. But matters were not resolved in Scotland and Mary was allowed to remain in England, though confined to one or other of Elizabeth's stately residences. The possibility of Mary joining one of the pro-Catholic movements being orchestrated against the crown in northern England was considered real. Instead of accepting her situation with grace, Mary began to plot against her cousin. She secretly supported the uprisings as well as various plans to assassinate Elizabeth. But not secretly enough. Elizabeth's Secretary of State William Cecil (now Lord Burghley) and his spymasters were monitoring signs of Catholic attempts on their queen's life. As Mary's implication in these became apparent, Cecil urged Elizabeth to action. Yet she hesitated. The final straw came in 1586 when Mary's role in Anthony Babington's assassination plot was revealed. On the first of February 1587, under pressure from her ministers, Elizabeth reluctantly signed her cousin's death warrant (in contrast to Catherine de Medici who herself deliberately started the Saint Bartholomew's Day massacre).

Like all successful statesmen, Elizabeth tried to avoid costly wars. She resisted the goading by Philip II of Spain as long as possible. But when his fleet arrived off the coast of Cornwall on 19 July 1588, Elizabeth had to act. On hearing the news, she made for Tilbury downstream from London where her ground troops were assembled. Her speech is well known (and considered apocryphal by many) but illustrates perfectly her success in promoting herself to her people: 'I am come among you at this time ... being resolved in the midst and heat of the battle to live and die amongst you all, to lay down for my God and my kingdom and for my people mine honour and my blood even in the dust. I know I have the body but of a weak and feeble woman, but I have the heart and stomach of a king ...' [13]. Fortunately the battle had already been won by the fire ships sent into the midst of the Spanish fleet, now off Calais, by Sir Francis Drake. But the winner was also the westerly gale that prevented the Spanish fleet from sailing into the estuary of the Thames.

Elizabeth made mistakes, a major one being to appoint Robert Devereux, Earl of Essex (whom she liked personally), to the head of her army. He was self-centred and incompetent as a leader. His campaign in Ireland in 1599 was a complete failure and he paid the price. Four years later the queen died. 'Few of those who knew her well ... were in any doubt that she was a creature of unusual intelligence, energy, determination and wisdom. ... She had a genuine affection for her subjects; a high sense of natural justice; loyalty to her friends and ministers; a profound awareness of her responsibilities; a devotion to duty' [14].

The 18th century was a period of relatively long reigns in Europe. Louis XV occupied the throne of France from 1715 to 1774, Frederick II that of Prussia from 1740 to 1786, George III that of Britain from 1760 to 1820, and Catherine II that of Russia from 1762 to 1796. So the time during which **Maria Theresa** (1717–1780) ruled her country, from 1740 to 1780, was not exceptional. What was remarkable was that this lady 'achieved for her realm of many lands a sort of balance, a synthesis, which was to enable it to survive into the twentieth century as a viable and more or less coherent society' [15]. Maria Theresa had a fairly lonely childhood and her education by Jesuits instilled more of a hatred for Protestants (and Jews) than a love of learning. Music and dancing were in her bones. At 19 she was married to Prince Francis Stephen of Lorraine with whom she had been in love since setting eyes on him a decade earlier. It proved a stable marriage and Maria Theresa's love for Francis never waned, despite his infidelities (that did not prevent him from siring 16 children with his wife). In 1740 her father, the Holy Roman Emperor Charles VI, died. He was succeeded as emperor by Charles VII, the son-in-law of his elder brother Emperor Joseph I. His other titles went to his eldest offspring, irrespective of gender, according to the Pragmatic Sanction that he had signed in 1713. Maria Theresa was now regnant Queen of Hungary, Bohemia (from 1743), Archduchess of Austria and holder of titles in many other Hapsburg lands. Two major problems faced her: Charles VI's realm was in poor financial state and the ever-scheming European nations saw an opportunity as soon as their hopes — that a women would succeed — were realised.

The first problem was exacerbated by a poor harvest. Maria Theresa did her best for the starving peasants by ordering all game, four-footed and feathered, on the vast Hapsburg hunting grounds to be killed and distributed to the people. It may have been only a gesture, but it was appreciated and remembered by the recipients. The second was more difficult. The advisors she inherited were incompetent and it would be some time before she could appoint men of her own choosing (which she would do with great success). Meanwhile Frederick II of Prussia, who had only just succeeded his own father, was the first off the mark. Barely a month after her father Charles VI's death, a Prussian envoy was in Vienna to propose a peace treaty with Austria that would 'be to her benefit'. Maria Theresa being heavily pregnant at the time, the mission was received by Francis. What the envoy did not reveal was that Frederick, at the head of 27,000 men, had already crossed the border into Silesia (the northeastern region of Austria). Austria's troops were scattered across the empire. Frederick's first success was at Mollwitz where a relatively small but well-trained army defeated an even smaller Austrian one which lacked artillery support as well as men. The War of the Austrian Succession, as the conflict with Prussia was to be called, would involve France, Spain, Bavaria and Saxony (that later switched sides) alongside Prussia, with Britain, Hanover and the Dutch

Republic supporting the Habsburgs. Not until 1748 would a peace treaty be signed. For Maria Theresa, who was being ceremoniously crowned as Queen of Hungary (on her own: the Hungarians would not recognise Stephen as co-regent; later they relented) in Pressburg [16] around the time of Mollwitz, it was a disastrous start to her reign. Worse was to follow. But an impassioned plea to the Hungarians for help had paid off: they supplied troops for her army and cash for her exchequer.

She was losing most of Silesia to Prussia and now, towards the end of 1741, was being attacked from the west by Charles Albert, Elector of Bavaria. A joint force of Bavarian and French troops entered Bohemia and were soon in Linz, then Prague. Vienna itself was threatened. Maria Theresa kept her nerve and refused to envisage a defeatist peace treaty. She replaced her husband Stephen, who had proved to be an ineffective commander, with Marshal Ludwig Khevenhüller. Under his leadership Austrian troops drove the Bavarians and French out of most of Bohemia and by February 1742 were in Munich — capital of Bavaria — itself. The war dragged on until the Peace of Aix-la-Chapelle in 1748. By this time the squabbles were far from Austrian soil — in the Netherlands and Italy — and Maria Theresa could devote time to her own family. Three years earlier she had accompanied Stephen to Frankfurt where he had been crowned Emperor (surprisingly with Frederick's own vote as Elector of Brandenburg). She was now Empress Consort, but gracefully refrained from being crowned by his side. In Vienna she appointed an unlikely man to be her chief advisor. He was a Portuguese nobleman, Don Manuel Count Tarouca, 20 years her elder. Tarouca would serve her faithfully, with sound advice and no concern for his own advancement, for the next 30 years. A typical day for Maria Theresa would begin with her rising at 8. 'After Mass, half an hour with the children. Then, from 9.30 to 12.30 it would be solid work: documents to read and initial, ministers to confer with, audiences to take. At 12.30 she was to stop everything, to relax before the midday meal at 12.45. ... After the meal an hour for herself, her children, her mother. ... More work sharp at 4 and right through to supper at 8.30. Seven and a half scheduled hours of work each day. Now she must relax, dance, play cards …' [17]. She kept herself fit by riding: like Catherine de Medici she was an ardent and experienced horsewoman.

Another war, the Seven Years War (1756–1765), was fought mainly between France and Britain and largely outside Europe altogether. Maria Theresa concentrated on reforming her realm. She unified the varying laws that existed throughout most of the Hapsburg lands, strengthened the army, founded the Viennese Medicine School, promoted vaccination against smallpox, and initiated compulsory, secular primary education. Her views of the Enlightenment were circumscribed. She distrusted religious emancipation, argued against any 'destruction of the nobility' and was 'too old to accommodate myself in such ideas' as 'liberty in everything' [18]. She lived to see her eldest son elected as Emperor Joseph II and her youngest daughter married to the Dauphin Louis of France (with unfortunate consequences). For 40 years she had done the best for her country. After her death following a chill caught during a pheasant shoot in pouring rain, it could truly be said that 'she had held her society together, encouraged its individual talents, and left it better than it was before' [19].

Catherine II of Russia (1729–1796) might be known as 'the Great', but Russian she was not. Moreover she was implicated in the plot to oust her husband Peter III, she prevented her son Paul from succeeding his father, she took lovers throughout her life and she grudged herself nothing in extravagant living. But she also proved to be the ablest, most enlightened person ever to govern Russia. Sophie Auguste Friderike, Princess of Anhalt-Zerbst, was born in Stettin some hundred miles northeast of Berlin. Like many a firstborn who is a girl, she was aware that her parents would have preferred a boy. Despite — or because of — this, Sophie's future life was dominated by two traits: ambition and determination. Early into her reign the Russian Empress Elizabeth, daughter of Peter I, started to look for a suitable wife for her likely successor, Karl Peter Ulrich, son of Elizabeth's sister Anna Petrovna. He was a year older than Sophie, and as Duke of Holstein her second cousin. Frederick the Great had recommended Sophie, so it is not too surprising that the empress invited Sophie's mother, Princess Johanna Elisabeth of Holstein-Gottorp, to bring her daughter to visit St Petersburg. On arrival Sophie encountered Peter, whom she had met five years earlier in Saxony. The young heir to the Russian throne, scarred by small pox, could not be considered anything but unimpressive and unattractive. Arrangements for Sophie's betrothal, preceded by her conversion from Lutherism to Orthodoxy, were soon underway and within months Sophie had become the Grand Duchess Yekaterina (Catherine) Alekseyevna. A year later Catherine and Peter, aged 16 and 17 respectively, were married. Following a banquet in the evening, Catherine was conducted to her bed 'not knowing what I was expected to do … Should I go to sleep? I knew nothing' [20]. After two hours her husband arrived and promptly fell asleep.

Matters did not improve over the years. Though they shared a bed they did not enjoy each other's company and began to seek satisfaction elsewhere. Catherine's waywardness was more serious in that it produced two miscarriages which she managed to conceal. The birth of a son, however, she announced with pride. Peter, Elizabeth and her court were delighted. Catherine herself was less convinced, which throws doubt on the supposed Romanov blood thought to have coursed through the veins of Paul I, Alexander I, Nicholas I, Alexander II, Alexander III and Nicholas II. On Christmas Day of 1761, Elizabeth died. The new tsar, Peter III, was popular with some, disliked by others. His physical and intellectual deficiencies were well known, and public humiliation of his wife the empress at a grand banquet was the spark that caused his opponents to act. Led by Prince Grigory Orlov (Catherine's lover, as it happens) they secured the support of the Guards Regiments and proclaimed Catherine Empress of Russia; her 8-year-old son Paul was ignored. The announcement was immediately supported by the Church and Peter dutifully abdicated. Four days later he was mortally wounded, most likely in a drunken brawl. His burial was simple, Catherine's coronation lavish.

The new empress' aim was to continue the modernisation of Russia that Peter I had initiated. Wooden palaces, churches and houses were rebuilt in stone. The beautifully curved Pavlovsk Palace [21] was built by Catherine for her son Paul. She bought paintings by well-known artists, such as Rembrandt's *Return of the Prodigal Son*, which she housed in a specially built gallery (now the Hermitage Museum). She promoted a Legislative Commission to define how the government should function, most of which was drafted by her: rising before 6 am she worked for two hours before her state secretary arrived at 8 am. Catherine collaborated with Ivan Betskoy on his *General Plan for the Education of Young People of Both Sexes* and founded two establishments for the education of girls [22]. Her attempt to abolish serfdom, however, failed. Catherine was a true enlightenment figure. She forged a friendship with Voltaire, whose library she bought at his death, and Diderot, whom she invited to St Petersburg. Another *philosophe*, the German Friedrich-Melchior Grimm, attended her son Paul's wedding to Sophia Dorothea of Württemberg. He considered Catherine to be 'a charming woman, the like of whom is not to be found in Paris', who talked 'often very gaily about serious things, and very seriously about frivolous things' [23]. Her championship of women is well illustrated by her appointment of Princess Dashkova as director of the Academy of Sciences that was founded by Peter I. 'It was a tribute to Catherine's perception and to her disregard for current prejudices, that she appointed a woman to take charge of an institution regarded as a male preserve' [24].

Catherine was lucky in war, in part because she appointed able military commanders who served her well. Conflict between Russia and Turkey had been rumbling on since the 16th century and would continue to do so into the 19th. During the Seventh Russo-Turkish War of 1768–1774, a dashing Prince Grigory Potëmkin, who subsequently became Catherine's lover — possibly husband — had distinguished himself at the battle of Larga in 1770. On the same day Alexei Orlov, Commander-in-Chief of the Russian navy and brother of Grigory, won a decisive naval battle at Chesma in the Aegean. The war ended with Russia being allowed to annex the peninsula of Crimea [25]. The following year Potëmkin put an end to a Cossack revolt, led by the charismatic Yemelyan Pugachev, which threatened the very government in St Petersburg. During the iniquitous carve-up of Poland by Austria, Prussia and Russia in 1772 and again in 1793, Catherine gained a large chunk in the east of the country: Peter the Great would have been proud of her. On the morning of 5 November (Old Style) 1796, having had a good night's sleep, Catherine suffered a stroke. She died the following day. Catherine proved that a foreigner — and a woman at that — could rule Russia better than any man to date.

Enlightenment and the Age of Reason

'In the later seventeenth and early eighteenth century the two major words banded about so frequently in debate were the words "reason" and "nature" ... a man's views had to be reasonable for them to be taken seriously, and the ultimate source of knowledge lay in erecting reasonable suppositions and arguments on the basis of hard fact culled from observations of the natural world' [26]. Philosophers argued about liberty and religion, scientists studied nature. Isaac Newton showed why the planets move as they do, Antoine van Leeuwenhoek discovered organisms too small to be seen with the naked eye: microbes. In his second *Discours* published in 1755, Jean-Jacques Rousseau suggested that primates [27] and primitive humans were somehow related, thus anticipating Charles Darwin by a century. What few considered worthy of study or debate was the inferior status of women. A lone voice during the 17th century had actually suggested that 'women do excel men in virtues and rare endowments of the minde, and I think we shall finde therein also women do farr outstrip men' [28]. But no one appears to have been listening.

Nevertheless several women were able to counter the androcentrism of the 17th century and realise their potential. One was Mary Beale (1633–1690), 'the first professional woman painter of Great Britain' [29]. She was fortunate in that her husband, himself an aspiring artist, accepted her superior talent and was happy to act as her assistant and manager. Although her fame was outshone by her contemporary the Flemish-born court painter Sir Peter Lely, she obtained commissions from, among others, the Duke of Devonshire, the Duchess of Newcastle and the Secretary of State Henry Coventry, as well as from two of Charles II's mistresses, Barbara Villiers and Nell Gwynn. Lady Penelope Harvey sat for both Lely and Beale. Lely makes her more attractive, but Beale's version is considered truer to life. In fact it now appears that several of Mary Beale's creations may have been incorrectly attributed to Peter Lely. Beale was a true

Enlightenment figure, taking time off her art to write an essay entitled *Discourse on Friendship* (1667). In it she 'affirms the capacity of a woman to respond to the demands of friendship, to forge a relationship that is both sympathetic and empathic, within marriage as well as outside, with a person of the same sex or of the other' [30].

Several ladies in France described courtly life, as Murasaki Shikibu had done 600 years earlier. Madame de Motteville is of particular interest as she gives us an insight into the nature of the young Louis XIV before he developed the hauteur of his later years. As his mother was dying, the 28–year-old 'helped her always with unbelieving application, he helped to change her bed, and served her better and more adroitly than all her women' [31].

The Puritan settlers who arrived in Massachusetts aboard the *Arbella* in 1630 included a young couple, Simon and Anne Bradstreet. She combined bearing eight children with writing *The Tenth Muse Lately Sprung Up in America*, a collection of poems considered to be the first English work to be published in America. Two decades later there arrived the Rev Joseph Rowlandson with his wife Mary. She was unfortunate enough to be captured, along with her three children one of whom died in captivity, by a group of Native Americans and held prisoner for almost three months. Six years after being ransomed and reunited with her husband she settled down to write *The Sovereignty and Goodness of God: Being a Narrative of the Captivity and Restoration of Mrs Mary Rowlandson*. This was so successful on both sides of the Atlantic that it was reprinted four times in its first year.

The English theatre, home to Shakespeare, Marlowe and Ben Jonson, produced few women playwrights during the Elizabethan era, but during the Restoration [32] period two women stood out. They were Aphra Behn and Delarivier Manley. A good account of the first is given in Jenni Murray's *A History of Britain in 21 Women* [33], while all of Manley's works may be read in a modern edition that also assesses their significance [34].

Not until the latter half of the 18th century did two English philosophers address the biased standing of women. Jeremy Bentham (1748–1832) was a child prodigy, learning Latin at the age of three and performing on the violin at seven. Educated at Westminster School and Queen's College, Oxford, he was trained as a lawyer. Instead of spending his life interpreting dry legal matters, he proposed reforms that astounded his audience: the separation of church and state, the abolition of slavery and the death penalty, the decriminalising of homosexual acts, equal rights for women, and more [35]. Bentham was a true Enlightenment figure. The other was Mary Wollstonecraft (1759–1797). She received little education and after her father lost all his money she had to fend for herself. She took a situation as companion to a lady in fashionable Bath. This resulted in *Thoughts on the Education of Daughters*. Eventually she found employment with a London bookseller, Joseph Johnson, who also published the works of men like Thomas Malthus, Erasmus Darwin (grandfather of Charles), Joseph Priestley and other Enlightenment figures. These now included Mary herself. She visited revolutionary France and was impressed by the movement. When the influential politician Edmund Burke published his criticism of the regime, she responded with *Vindication of the Rights of Men* (1790). This led seamlessly to *A Vindication of the Rights of Woman* two years later. The reforms proposed by Bentham and Wollstonecraft would have to wait almost a century before being seriously considered by politicians able to implement some of their radical ideas.

Women had been working on scientific issues for some time. Marie Meurdrac wrote a treatise on chemistry especially for women, *La Chymie charitable et facile en faveur des dames*, that was published in Paris in 1666. Among other achievements, Gabrielle Emelie Le Tonnelier de Breteuil translated Newton's *Principia* into French. The *philosophe* Voltaire called her 'a great man whose only fault was in being a woman' [36], which he proved by taking her as his lover. In England Caroline Herschel (1750–1848), using her brother William's telescope when he was away, discovered five new comets on her own. Anne Paulzer Lavoisier (1758–1836) translated English articles on 'phlogiston' theory into French for her husband Antoine. These were crucial to his rejection of the theory and his consequential discovery of the element oxygen. None of these women received the recognition that was their due. In the case of Caroline Herschel and Anne Lavoisier it was their male partners who were feted.

But one lady who bucked the trend was the Italian Maria Gaetana Agnesi (1718–1799), daughter of the Professor of Mathematics at the

University of Bologna. Maria inherited her father's flair and produced the first compendium of mathematics that explained the theories of Leibniz and Newton. It was translated into English and remained the standard mathematical treatise for the next 50 years. She also wrote 190 essays on subjects ranging from philosophy and logic to mechanics and Newton's theory of gravity. Her *Propositiones Philosophicae* 'was a plea for the education of women' [37]. Agnesi's contributions were recognised in 1778 when she was elected to the Bologna Academy of Sciences that had been founded in 1690. But this was an exception. National Academies were far behind — except in Russia as mentioned earlier.

L'Académie Française, established in 1635, elected its first female member in 1980 (Margaret Yourcenar). The Royal Society, founded in 1660, elected its first female members (Kathleen Lonsdale and Marjory Stephenson) in 1945. And in case you were wondering, the National Academy of Science in the USA, founded in 1863, did not elect its first woman until 1924 (Florence Sabin). Even today only 12% of science academy members globally are women. When in 1903 Marie Curie won the Nobel Prize for Physics (the first woman ever to win a Nobel) together with her husband and Henri Becquerel, the *New York Herald* could still say that Marie Curie 'is a devoted fellow-labourer in her husband's researches and has associated her name with his discoveries' [38a], which was entirely untrue and a gross calumny.

Just as this book was going to press, writer Nina Galbart's *Minerva's French Sisters* appeared [38b]. In it she describes the achievements of six Enlightenment French women. One of the best known is a botanist, Jeanne Baret (1740–1807), who became the first woman to circumnavigate the world. In order to achieve this she adopted male attire and called herself Jean. Another is novelist, chemist and writer on putrefaction, Geneviève Thiroux d'Arconville (1720–1805). She did not put her name to her works. As Virginia Woolf would later say, 'For most of history, Anonymous was a woman.'

One of the leading philosophers during the 18th century was Immanuel Kant. In his essay 'What Is Enlightenment?' (1784) he wrote 'Dare to know! Have courage to use your own reason!' The words were not lost on

18-year-old Anne-Louise Germaine Necker, better known today as **Madame de Staël** (1766–1817). The Neckers' only child, she grew up in an affluent household that shuttled between their residence in Paris, a country house at St Ouen, and a noble villa at Coppet on the shore of Lake Geneva. Mme Necker allowed Germaine to attend her weekly salon in Paris from an early age, which must have influenced the young girl's love of learning, wit and repartee. At her mother's salon she met Voltaire and Rousseau. At her own she would entertain and stimulate the cream of Europe's intellectuals over more than 30 years. At 12 years of age she entered the marriage market. Her parents would appraise potential husbands, all of whom were aware of Germaine's considerable dowry. A Swedish diplomat, in severe financial difficulties due to his gambling debts, was the first to approach M Necker. It took seven years for Erik Magnus Staël von Holstein to emerge victorious. None of the three children Germaine would produce over the next 11 years was her husband's.

Beauty is not essential to attract a man. In Mme de Staël's case it was her conversation and her eccentric nature that no man on whom she had set her sights could resist. Except the recently returned conqueror of Italy. Bonaparte disliked intelligent (and plain) women, and the lady's polemics on freedom and liberty were at odds with his own ambitions. The royalist press, too, was antagonistic: 'She writes on metaphysics which she does not understand, on morality which she does not practice, on the virtues of her sex which she lacks' [39]. She decided to quit France and visit Weimar and Berlin. She was accompanied by her three children and her latest lover Benjamin Constant, who spoke fluent German and acted as 'tutor'. To him she was simply 'the most famous person of our age through her writing and her conversation' [40]. They were entertained by the Grand Duke of Saxe-Weimar who introduced Mme de Staël to Schiller, Herder and Goethe. The latter would praise her '*De l'Allemagne*', which within three days of publication would be sold out. In Berlin she met the philosopher Fichte, a disciple of Kant.

On her return she was placed under house arrest following the French defeat of the Swiss in 1798 and retired to her Swiss home. Here the Coppet Group of writers, philosophers and politicians became one of the most active and influential in Europe. 'All believed passionately in the value of litérature ... in a spirit of freedom and mutual respect' [41]. Her salon became the focus for Europe's intelligentsia. 'There are three great powers in Europe: England, Russia and Madame de Staël' [42], it was said. Her literary output was eclectic: essays, commentaries, novels, books on literary topics (she practically invented comparative literature), politics and travel, as well as plays. Her fundamental standpoint is perhaps best summed up in her own words: 'Liberty is nothing other than morality in government' [43]. Many of the traits exhibited by Mme de Staël and by the four Queens introduced earlier — scheming and ruthlessness, vision and leadership — would have been considered as typically male by most men of the time. The two sexes are indeed innately similar in this regard.

Telling stories to one's children has always been an accepted role for women to play. Not surprising then that female novelists appear to have avoided androcentric criticism better than writers of history or philosophy. Indeed, 'by 1847 some women writers were accepted well enough for a literary magazine to suggest that the young Anthony Trollope might change his surname so as to avoid comparison with his famous literary mother' [44].

Revolutions

Androcentrism was so ingrained in 18th-century society that the exhortations for liberty by Thomas Paine might not have seemed hypocritical to Abigail Adams. Dutifully she would pack sandwiches for the first leg of yet another long journey south by her beloved husband John. Nor would he, the mild-mannered student of Harvard College and now budding lawyer, have envisaged that within 20 years he would become the second president of a United States of America. So it is not surprising that no woman was among the delegates from the 13 colonies (Connecticut, Delaware, Georgia, Maryland, Massachusetts Bay, New Hampshire, New Jersey, New York, North Carolina, Pennsylvania, Rhode Island, South Carolina and Virginia) who signed the United States Declaration of Independence in Philadelphia on 4 July 1776. Likewise, women were not present at the drafting of the

Constitution of the United States two years later. Abraham Lincoln's fine words at Gettysburg in 1863 about the 'inalienable Rights' of men in regard to 'Life, Liberty and the pursuit of Happiness' did not extend to females. Not until the 19th Amendment to the United States Constitution was passed in August of 1920 were women granted citizenship and the right to vote.

The situation in France was not so different. 'Without question, women never enjoyed equal political participation in the French Revolution with their fellow men. The Declaration of the Rights of Man and the Citizen (1789) and the constitution of 1791 excluded women and other sectors of society from formal participation in the articulation of the laws of the new regime' [45]. The Law on Divorce of 1792 made it easier for a woman to divorce her husband [46]. But so far as other aspects of *liberté*, *égalité* and *fraternité* are concerned, French women had to wait until 1945 in order to gain the vote.

Victorian England

The country may have prospered during the 19th century under a female monarch for more than 60 years, but for all except upper-class women life was grim. In order to put food on the table for her family, an impoverished woman might have to work from 6 am to 7 pm in a factory. Her salary would be a third to a half that of a man, which itself was barely adequate. Prior to the Mines and Collieries Act of 1842 that forbade the employment of women and girls underground, half-naked women were pulling heavy carts of coal below the surface for up to 12 hours a day. Middle-class women did not face such atrocious conditions but their lives were restricted in other ways. 'If married, a woman could own no property. She had no right to any earnings she might make. She could not make a will. She had no separate existence in law. She could not conclude contracts or leases with another party. If she attempted to flee her husband, he had the legal right to enter the property of anyone harbouring her, and remove her by force. ... She could not sue for divorce, however atrociously her husband behaved' [47].

The Enlightenment views of Bentham and Wollstonecraft attracted thinkers who were in a position to do something about them. 'The most influential English language philosopher of the nineteenth century' [48] was John Stuart Mill (1806–1873). His *On Liberty* (1859) would be followed by *The Subjugation of Women* [49]. His views were clear. '"The legal subordination of one sex to another", he wrote, "is now wrong in itself, and now one of the chief hindrances to human improvement"' [50]. Mill was elected a Member of Parliament for the City of Westminster in 1865. He collected over 1,500 signatures in support of a bill on women's suffrage. This he presented to Parliament on 7 June, speaking on its behalf on 17 July 1866. A year later the Second Reform Act was passed. This gave the vote to all householders who were, by definition, male. Mill proposed an amendment to make the qualification independent of the sex of the individual. It was defeated by 194 votes to 73. Calls for the enfranchisement of women rumbled on, but it would take another 51 years before a majority in Parliament agreed to this proposition, as described in the following chapter.

Notes

1. see https://en.wikipedia.org/wiki/Estimates_of_historical_world_population
2. see https://en.wikipedia.org/wiki/Life_expectancy
3. see https://ourworldindata.org/child-mortality-in-the-past
4. Frieda (2005), p 36.
5. Philip II succeeded the Spanish throne in 1556 when his father Charles V abdicated as Holy Roman Emperor and divided the Hapsburg lands between Spain and his German-speaking nations; the title of Holy Roman Emperor passed to Charles' brother Ferdinand of Austria.
6. the marriage had been proposed by Henry II at the death of her father, James V of Scotland, and Mary had been brought to France aged five to be imbued with the intricacies of French court life. Her mother Marie, daughter of Charles Duke of Guise, had remained in Scotland as Queen Regent. The young Mary was now queen consort of France as well as queen of Scotland. But the throne she coveted was that of England.
7. so-called after a meeting of Protestants in the village of Hugues.

8. Frieda (2005), pp 456 and 454 respectively.

9. *ibid*, p 221.

10. according to a poll in a television debate held in Britain in 2005. Note that the next two monarchs — out of a total of 12 — were also women: Victoria and Elizabeth II.

11. Johnson (1974), p 18.

12. Loades (2003), p 142.

13. Leah S Marcus, Janet Mueller and Mary Beth Rose (eds): *Elizabeth I: Collected Works* (Chicago: University of Chicago Press, 2000) and considered by the editors to be authentic.

14. Johnson (1974), p 442.

15. Crankshaw (1969), p 5.

16. on the Danube, a short distance downstream from Vienna. Then the capital of Hungary, it was replaced in 1873 by Budapest even further downstream. Pressburg, today called Bratislava, is now the capital of Slovakia.

17. Crankshaw (1969), p 113.

18. Parsons (2008), p 176.

19. Crankshaw (1969), p 338.

20. Dixon (2009), p 63.

21. near Tsarskoe Selo (Tsar's Village), 30 km south of St Petersburg. Now called Pushkin after the poet who had a house here, it is home to the grand Catherine Palace. This was originally a smaller structure built for Catherine I. It was replaced by the empress Elizabeth, with further embellishments of palace and gardens by Catherine II.

22. the Smolny Institute for daughters of the nobility and the Novodeichii Institute for those of humbler origin.

23. Dixon (2009), p 222.

24. Isabel de Madariaga: *Russia in the Age of Catherine the Great* (London: Weidenfeld and Nicolson, 1981), quoted in Dixon (2009), p 264.

25. as President Putin would do in 2014 without any peace treaty.

26. Redwood (1976), p 12.

27. today the word includes humans, apes and monkeys.

28. from a manuscript that came to light a few decades ago and was quoted in the *Daily Telegraph* (April 20, 2002).

29. my translation of Renaud (2010), p 128.

30. *ibid*, p 91.

31. taken from Philip Mansel: *Women Writers of the French Court* (London Library Magazine, Winter 2019, issue 46, pp 20–23).

32. of Charles II in 1660 following his exile in France.
33. Jenni Murray: *A History of Britain in 21 Women* (London: Oneworld, 2016), pp 37–46.
34. Rachel Carnell, ed: *The Selected Works of Delarivier Manley* (London: Pickering and Chatto, 2005).
35. see https://intriguing-history.com/jeremy-bentham-advocates-womens-suffrage/
36. Alic (1986), p 139.
37. *ibid*, p 137.
38a. Quinn (1999), p 193.
38b. Nina Rattner Gelbart: *Minerva's French Sisters* (Connecticut: Yale University Press, 2021).
39. Fairweather (2005), p 251.
40. *ibid*, p 1.
41. *ibid*, p 331.
42. *ibid*, p 3.
43. *ibid*, p 473.
44. Victoria Glendinning: *Trollope* (London: Pimlico Press, 1993), p 166.
45. Colm Ó Conaill: *Women and Divorce Legislation: A Quest for Liberty During the French Revolution*, in Meek and Lawless (2005), p 195.
46. *ibid*, p 209.
47. Heffer (2014), p 506.
48. Stanford Encyclopedia of Philosophy Archive, Spring 2017 Edition.
49. London: Longmans, Green, Reader and Dyer, 1869.
50. Heffer (2014), p 568.

Chapter 7

Decline: The 20th Century

During the Covid-19 lockdown in early 2020 I have been taking a walk through Brompton Cemetery (a kind of dry-run). At this time of year it is full of wild bluebells, primulas and other spring flowers. Most of the graves, which span nigh on two centuries, lie bare. Except one, which has fresh flowers on it every time I pass. It is dedicated 'to the memory of Emmeline Pankhurst, wife of R M Pankhurst'. Emmeline Goulden, who at 21 years of age married the 45-year-old Richard Pankhurst, had become interested in women's rights since her teenage years in Manchester, where she was born in 1858. Together with her daughter Christabel she campaigned vigorously for women's suffrage, smashing windows, assaulting policemen and going on hunger strike during the ensuing prison sentences. In 1914 she halted all such activities in order to support her country in the war against Germany. In 1999 *Time* magazine's list of the 100 most important people of the 20th century, more than 80 of whom were men, included Pankhurst alongside Coco Chanel, Rachel Carson, Diana Princess of Wales, Anne Frank, Helen Keller, Marilyn Monroe, Rosa Parkes, Mother Teresa and Margaret Thatcher. But she was not the first of the suffragettes.

Women had been agitating for voting rights since the middle of the 19th century, with little effect. The first countries in which women's suffrage was achieved were in fact small islands under the nominal control of more powerful neighbours. These were the Pitcairn Isles, where the female descendants of men from the *Bounty* won this privilege in 1838. Next came Hawaii in 1840 (but repealed 12 years later), followed by the (perhaps inappropriately named) Isle of Man in 1881. In Britain, of which the Isle of Man is a part but without representation at Westminster, the efforts of

Emmeline Pankhurst and her fellow suffragettes were finally rewarded. The Representation of the People Act was passed by Parliament in February of 1918. Any man aged 21 now had the vote, irrespective of whether he was a householder or not. For women, the householder — or wife of householder — qualification remained. Moreover, they had to be over 30 (until a further Act in 1928 made the qualification the same as for men). But it was a momentous step forward. 40% of adult women were no longer disenfranchised.

Following the 1918 Act two women, one of fortitude the other of fortune, would even become Members of Parliament. The first was Constance Markiewicz, an Irish nationalist and member of Sinn Féin married to a Polish 'count'. In the general election of 14 December 1918 she was returned for the constituency of Dublin St Patrick's, which was then part of the Westminster parliament. But she did not take her seat because members of Sinn Féin refuse to swear allegiance to the British crown (she was, in any case, in Holloway Prison at the time). Markiewicz subsequently served in the Irish Dáil as a Cabinet Minister. The other woman was the American-born Nancy Astor. Her husband Waldorf had been MP for Plymouth Sutton until he became Viscount Astor on the death of his father in 1919. The parliamentary seat was now vacant and Nancy decided to contest it at a by-election in November 1919. The voters dutifully elected her. Of the many quips said to have been exchanged between Nancy Astor and Winston Churchill, who had opposed women's suffrage, most are considered apocryphal. The 'If you were my husband, I'd put poison in your coffee', 'If you were my wife, I'd drink it' was probably made by Churchill's friend F. E. Smith, Lord Birkenhead [1]. In 1930 Smith published a book in which he said, 'In 2030 women will still, by their wit and charms, inspire the most able men towards heights that they could never themselves achieve' [2]. 'In 1958, a fund was launched to set up Churchill College, Cambridge, which would concentrate on science and technology. ... (Churchill) wanted the college to admit women on equal terms with men. "When I think what women did in the war", he said, "I feel sure they deserve to be treated equally". It might also be seen as a belated apology for his short-sighted opposition to female suffrage forty years earlier' [3].

The college was the first all-male college to decide to accept women, which it did in 1972.

The acceptance of women as professionals in public life was slow to develop in Britain. 'In 1900 there were nearly 2 million in domestic service, but only 200 female doctors and two architects' [4]. During World War II women began to occupy leadership roles. In the USA, Mary Anderson had been appointed Director of the Women's Bureau of the Department of Labor in 1920 and she continued in that role until 1944. Mary Pillsbury Lord served as Assistant Regional Director of the Office of Civilian Defense and in 1944 was appointed chairman of the National Civilian Advisory Committee of the Women's Army Corps. Ellen Sullivan Woodward was one of three members of the Social Security Board from 1938 to 1946 [5].

Politicians

As chronicled in this book, there have on occasion been female monarchs since pharaonic times. Only in the second half of the 20th century, though, did women politicians, like *Galanthus nivalis* pushing its way through the snow, begin to emerge as leaders of their country. I will describe them in order of becoming leader. All shared three qualities essential for successful leadership: judgement, determination and fortitude.

The first female leader was **Sirimavo Bandaranaike** (1916–2000). Sirima (the -vo is a mark of respect that she earned during her political career) was descended from the 15th-century ruling family of Kandy on the island of **Ceylon**. At 24 she married Solomon Bandaranaike, a respected politician whose political career she supported when not engaged in social work on behalf of disadvantaged women and girls in rural areas. Solomon became prime minister in 1957 but was assassinated by a Buddhist monk two years later. Sirima now entered politics and within ten months had moved seamlessly from prime minister's widow to **prime minister** herself in **1957**. She proved to be a wily politician and won two more elections (1965 and 1970). The country had already gained independence (of the UK) in 1948, but Bandaranaike steered it to become the Republic of

Sri Lanka in 1972. She lost the election in 1977 and spent the next 12 years in opposition. A stubborn woman, she continued to campaign and won again in 1989 and 1994. In 2000, aged 84, she resigned. Two months later she died of a heart attack. Bandaranaike was not only the first female prime minister in the world, but also one of the longest holders of that office.

The subcontinent was host to another female politician. **Indira Gandhi** (1917–1984) was the daughter of Jawaharlal Nehru, first prime minister of the newly independent **India**. With her father occasionally in prison (for promoting resistance to British rule) and her mother bedridden with tuberculosis much of the time, Indira's childhood was an unhappy one. But as mentioned before, this can bring future success in a female of fortitude. At the age of 20 she went to study at Oxford's Somerville College, but ill health forced her to leave without taking her degree. No matter: she received an Honorary Doctorate in 1971. While in England, she met her future husband Feroze Gandhi (no relation to the Mahatma). Indira worked for her father during his premiership and served as president of the Congress party before being appointed to the Rajya Sabha, the Indian parliament's upper house, in 1964. The politicians thought that being a woman, they could bend her to their will. Too late they discovered they were dealing with a rod of steel. Gandhi became **prime minister** in **1966** and remained in office for the next 11 years. She veered towards socialism, nationalising many leading banks and promoting anti-poverty programmes in favour of India's huge underclass. Yet she was staunchly anti–communist and had backed the removal of the Kerala State Government in 1959. In 1971 India won a short war against Pakistan and Gandhi was instrumental in creating the nation of Bangladesh to replace East Pakistan, for which she was hailed as a goddess by the locals (and the opposite by Pakistanis).

Autocratic leaders invite opposition. Gandhi was accused of irregularities in her election win in Uttar Pradesh of 1971, and blamed for rising inflation (caused largely by the oil crisis of 1973). Calls for her resignation and removal from office followed. These she swept aside and instead ordered a State of Emergency. This gave the police powers of arrest and Gandhi used these to oust most of her political opponents. But her support was waning and she lost the election of 1977. The incoming government ordered her arrest which she avoided by appealing to the courts. The case rumbled on, during which time the government began to lose the support of the people. It lost the election of 1980 and Gandhi was swept to power once more. Her policy of even-handedness was a successful one. She would foster a trade deal with the Soviet leader Leonid Brezhnev one day, host a (British) Commonwealth Heads of Government meeting on another, and discuss nuclear disarmament with US president Ronald Reagan on a third. But it was not to last. On 30 October 1984 she was shot leaving her home by two of her own (Sikh [6]) security guards. A poll conducted by the UK's BBC in 1999 named her as the most influential woman, not of the century, but of the millennium.

Golda Mabovitch (1898–1978) was born in Kiev. Her father emigrated to the United States when Golda was five. Work in the railyard of Milwaukee enabled him to bring the rest of the family out a year later. In the US Golda became a convinced Zionist. She met her future husband, Morris Meyerson, on a trip to Denver and in 1917 they married with the intention of moving to Palestine. The entry of the US into the war pre-vented this and it was not until 1921 that **Golda Meir** [7] achieved her ambition of living and working in a kibbutz alongside her husband. Her political life took off when she was elected to the Working Women's Council, on whose behalf she spent two years back in the US as an emissary. In 1938 Meir travelled to France as an observer at the Évian conference summoned by US President Roosevelt to discuss the plight of Jews in Nazi Germany. Of the 32 nations represented at the conference, all of whom expressed their sorrow and concern, only the Dominican Republic offered to accept some into its country. Unlike the ladies of Philadelphia and Paris in the 1770s, in 1948 Golda was one of two female signatories of the Declaration of Independence by **Israel**.

She spent a year and a half in the Soviet Union as Minister Plenipotentiary. It was a delicate mission. Israel wanted to purchase arms from Eastern Europe to defend itself, while Stalin was looking to exert influence in the Middle East without abandoning his antipathy towards religious institutions (antipathy won out). On return from Moscow Golda Meir was appointed Minister of Labour. Her programme was a hugely successful one of building houses, hospitals, schools and roads, as well as promoting industrial and agricultural projects. Appointed Foreign Minister in 1956, she lent her support to African nations seeking independence, but discouraged sick and handicapped Polish Jews from migrating to Israel. During this time she was diagnosed with mild lymphoma and she resigned from the government. But her passion for politics soon brought her back and in **1969** she was appointed **prime minister**. She won two wars against her Arab neighbours: the Six-Day War of 1967 against Egypt, Jordan and Syria, and the Yom Kippur War of 1973 against Egypt and Syria. The following year Meir did something most politicians are unable to contemplate: she retired voluntarily, stating that five years had been enough. Her determination in holding her neighbours at bay was rewarded in 1977 when the Egyptian President Anwar Sadat became the first Arab leader to visit Israel in search of peace. The following year her lymphoma returned and she died in December of 1978. *Time* magazine had named her Woman of the Year in 1956 and in 1974 American Mothers, Inc. had awarded her the title of World Mother. Golda Meir's name is commemorated in schools, libraries and other cultural centres across Israel and in five American cities.

Margaret Thatcher (1925–2013), born Margaret Hilda Roberts, had a conventional childhood and early life, typical of any middle-class girl growing up in the **United Kingdom**. She read Chemistry at Oxford, arriving at Somerville College six years after Indira Gandhi. Her scientific background was put to good use: in her first job she developed a novel technology for making soft frozen ice cream. But her real interest, begun at Oxford, was in politics on the Conservative side. Having married Denis Thatcher, a successful businessman, she was able to follow her bent without financial worries. Her attempts to be elected to parliament (in a Labour-held seat) failed and she devoted herself to bringing up her young twin children. Within four years politics trumped motherhood. In 1959 she was elected to the safe seat of Finchley which she held for the rest of her political life. She was appointed Secretary of State for Education and Science, the first qualified scientist to hold that post, by prime minister Edward Heath. She repaid Heath by standing against him at the Conservative Leadership election of 1975 and winning. The first female leader of any party became **prime minister** by defeating Labour in the general election of **1979**. Thatcher espoused Friedrich Hayek's philosophy of a free market, which led 364 economists to oppose her policy. Asked in the House of Commons whether she could name anyone who agreed with her, she cited Patrick Minford and Alan Walters, 'but, it is said, she was relieved not to have been asked to name a third' [8]. Her scientific training meant that 'she was much more rigorous about evidence and facts than most politicians'. One of the first world leaders to draw attention to the danger of climate change, in 1988 Thatcher told the Royal Society that 'stable prosperity can be achieved throughout the world provided the environment is nurtured and safeguarded' [9].

She survived one assassination attempt but succumbed to another. The first was by the IRA, who detonated a bomb in the hotel in which she was staying for the party conference in 1984. The second, figuratively speaking, was by her own cabinet in 1990. She had foolishly introduced a poll tax (by which the owner of a grand mansion paid the same as one of a small apartment) and had lost the confidence of her own supporters. When she became prime minister the nation had been on the verge of bankruptcy. When she was deposed the country was recovering and a new spirit of optimism was abroad, but at a cost: unemployment had risen sharply. She had won a war against the invaders of the Falkland Islands, had promoted privatisation of industry and given council house tenants the opportunity to acquire their own home, had invigorated the financial sector, and seen off the unions that had brought down the Heath government. She was loved by Conservatives, loathed by the rest. Her strength of purpose led to the sobriquet of the 'Iron Lady'. The French president François Mitterand told her that she had the 'eyes of Caligula and the mouth of Marilyn Monroe'.

In 2000 a reporter covering the UN General Assembly Special Session to review progress since the 1995 Beijing Conference on Women asked five of the women leaders present [10] how it was that they had achieved such prominent positions within the UN system. Catherine Bertini answered for all when she replied that it was because her father had supported and encouraged her. This was certainly true of **Gro Harlem Brundtland**

(1939–). Gro was born in Oslo, **Norway**. While studying medicine at Oslo University she met her future husband Olav Brundtland. Their engagement was a surprise to many. Gro followed her father Gudmund Harlem, a Norwegian Labour cabinet minister, in her political views, whereas Olav was a staunch Conservative. Yet their marriage would prove to be one of the most successful of any political leader. Olav became the bedrock on whom Gro could depend — whether looking after their four children or ironing Gro's dress on her way to be appointed prime minister by the king. When Henry Kissinger met the Brundtlands in 1981 he commented, 'This would not work in the United States. The press would tear it apart' [11].

The advantage of a scientific or medical background is not difficult to discern in Gro's case. After being appointed Minister for Environment Affairs by Labour Prime Minister Trygve Bratelli in 1974, a journalist asked her: 'Do you really need a medical degree? As soon as these Harlems reach 30-something, they get drafted into government, always as the youngest member'. Gro responded: 'Social and political factors alone dictated my choice to study medicine. In my opinion, I am using my education much more effectively as a government Minister than I would have as a doctor' [12]. A year into her ministerial duties, Gro was elected as Deputy Leader of the Labour Party, and two years later as member of parliament for Oslo. She would take up her seat only after leaving office, as in Norway cabinet ministers do not sit in parliament (rather like the situation in the USA). In **1981**, to most people's surprise she was appointed **prime minister**. Her socialist policies were measured: 'It does not make sense to begin with the illusion that the state could simply distribute money to schools, day care, the health sector, private consumption and all other things on everybody's list of good wishes' [13]. A sensible recipe for leaders elsewhere. Labour lost the following election and while Gro was out of office UN Secretary-General Perez de Cuellar asked her to head a World Commission on Environment and Development, subsequently known as the Brundtland Commission. This would lead to the Earth Summit in Rio de Janeiro in 1992 and thence to the International Panel on Climate Change. Meanwhile in Norway the Conservative lost the 1986 election and Gro was back in office. In 1996 she became the youngest and first female to be elected to the post of Director-General of the World Health Organisation (WHO). The research programmes initiated by her — Roll Back Malaria and the Stop TB Initiative — remain among the most important of WHO's functions today. Not surprising that in 2004 the UK's *Financial Times* called her the fourth most influential European (behind Pope John Paul II, Michael Gorbachev and Margaret Thatcher).

Corazon Aquino (1933–2009), born Maria Corazon Sumulong Cojuangco, daughter of one prominent family in the **Philippines** entered another by marriage to Senator Anigno Aquino Jr. Her parents moved to the USA while Corazon was still a teenager. After high school in Philadelphia, she graduated from the College of Mount Saint Vincent in New York City. She returned to the Philippines in 1953 where she met and married Anigno Aquino, whose political aspirations she supported financially. She also presented him with five children, one of whom would become president in 2010. Anigno was a bold politician in his criticism of the powerful and autocratic President Ferdinand Marcos, as a result of which he was jailed for eight years, after which the Aquino family left the country. After three years in Boston, which Corazon later considered to have been the happiest in her life, Anigno returned to Manila alone. His feet had barely touched ground when he was shot in the head. Several people were arrested, all subsequently acquitted. Corazon returned to lead her husband's funeral procession and avenge his murder. A million people urged her to stand for the presidency in a snap election called by Marcos in 1986. She agreed, but the votes were rigged against her. By this time even the military had had enough and confirmed Corazon's inauguration as **president** on 25 February **1986**. By nightfall Marcos had fled the country.

Reforming the country after two decades of cronyism and corruption under Marcos was not easy. She tried hard to mend the economy and managed to reduce the country's debt somewhat. She initiated agrarian and democratic reforms. Her presidency was not helped by natural disasters: an earthquake, the second largest volcanic eruption of the 20th century, and a devastating typhoon. Aquino ploughed on determinedly. When her stipulated six years in office were up she respectfully stepped down and devoted the rest of her life to promoting the Philippines on the international stage.

Time magazine rightly listed her among the 20 most influential Asians of the 20th century. Her tenacity in restoring the Philippine's standing was recognised by 16 universities across the world with an honorary doctorate. In 2008 Corazon Aquino was diagnosed with colorectal cancer. She died the following year.

Like Indira Gandhi, **Benazir Bhutto** (1953–2007) was born into a prominent political family. Her life would follow her father's in several regards: an Oxford education (he Christ Church, she Lady Margaret Hall after study at Radcliffe College in the US), prime minister of **Pakistan** and death after leaving office (execution and assassination respectively). On return to Pakistan her ambition to enter public life was scotched when her father was arrested on a dubious charge of murder and eventually condemned to death by hanging. Benazir spent the next five years in and out of prison before being deported in 1984. During her three-year exile she spent time in London, visited the United States, the Soviet Union and addressed the European Parliament in Strasbourg. Back in Pakistan, she agreed to marry her mother's choice of husband: Asif Ali Zardari, a wealthy businessman; Benazir retained her family surname. She campaigned to move the Pakistan People's Party (PPP) towards free market capitalism, as her admired Margaret Thatcher had done in Britain, and, despite Islamic opposition to a female **prime minister**, won in **1988**. She was the first (and only) woman leader in any Islamic country. At 35 she was also the youngest.

Bhutto improved relations with India, but her attempts to move Pakistan towards a more civic society — though she showed her respect for Islam by two religious trips to Mecca — failed. She tried to meet the high unemployment rate and the country's financial woes by approaching the United States. Unbeknown to her was Pakistan's programme to achieve nuclear capability that the military was conducting in secrecy. The CIA, of course, was well aware of this and US policy was firmly against supplying aid while the country was thus engaged. She was, however, invited to address a joint session of Congress. Charges of corruption against Bhutto's husband, in which she was also involved, led to her dismissal by President Ghulam Khan. The PPP lost the ensuing elections but in 1993 was back in government with Bhutto as prime minister. She encouraged the appointment of women to senior positions in government, the civil service and the law, right up to the Supreme Court, and tried to retard the nuclear programme as much as possible. Charges of corruption in her administration stuck and President Farooq Leghari dismissed the government. Bhutto was again in opposition. Worse was to come. Switzerland accused her of money laundering and she spent much time abroad refuting these accusations. She also wrote her last book [14]. In 2007 she returned to Pakistan to resume her political career. On 27 December she was leaving a PPP rally in Rawalpindi in her bulletproof (but open) car and decided to stand up to wave to the crowds. An assassin fired three shots and detonated his suicide vest, killing more than 20 people. Benazir was one of them. She was celebrated abroad, censured at home. Benazir's public life was a troubled one but her determination shone through. Stamps and a memorial coin have borne her head and hospitals, roads, universities and Islamabad International Airport have been named after her (the latter honour perhaps intended to mark her frequent departures).

Politicians' blood runs through the veins of **Chandrika Kumaratunga** (1945–): both her parents, Solomon and Sirimavo Bandaranaike (see above), served as prime minister of **Sri Lanka**. Chandrika spent most of her 20s in France, studying politics and economics. On return to Sri Lanka she became active in the Sri Lanka Freedom Party (SLFP) that was founded by her father and led by her mother after the former's assassination. Two years as consultant for the Food and Agricultural Organisation of the United Nations were followed by marriage to Vijaya Kumaratunga, a popular film star and then himself a politician. But not for long. Having formed his own Sri Lanka Mahajana (SLMP) party he fell into disfavour with the army and leadership of the country and was assassinated in 1988. Chandrika saw the writing on the wall and left for the UK. Two years later she felt able to return to the violent politics of Sri Lanka. Two of her political rivals having been assassinated, she campaigned for leadership of the SLFP and the premiership. She was appointed **prime minister** in August **1994**, with her mother in the cabinet. Chandrika contested the election for **president** in October of that year and won. She became the first female president of any country, and probably the only one ever to appoint her mother to the premiership (Sirimavo Bandaranaike's third term). Chandrika's terms as president (1994–1999 and 1999–2005) were dominated by civil war against the Tamil Tigers' separatist movement. She managed to hold the country together throughout this difficult time, though it cost her the use of her right eye from a botched assassination attempt by the Tigers. Now retired, her legacy as a politician of enormous determination is undeniable.

Jennifer Mary Robson (1952–), called Jenny, was born in Southland which, as the name implies, is on the southern tip of South Island in **New Zealand**. She was educated locally and attended Christchurch College of Education. This qualified her for an educational career and she became a primary school teacher, during which time she met and married Burton Shipley. The only whiff of political ambition that disturbed the early life of **Jenny Shipley** was to join the centre-right National Party. In her mid-30s she changed tack and stood for parliament in the safe National seat of Ashburton. Her political abilities were soon recognised and she served as Minister of Social Welfare, then Minister of Health in the cabinet of prime minister Jim Bolger. Following Margaret Thatcher, she challenged the man who had given her political office by standing against him in an election for the leadership of her party and winning. Bolger resigned and Jenny Shipley became New Zealand's first female **prime minister** in **1997**. Her premiership was too brief for her to be able to initiate major reforms. She supported gay and lesbian issues, lowered the legal age for alcohol purchases from 20 to 18, hosted the Asia-Pacific Economic Cooperation, and supported the monarchy over republicanism. She lost the 1999 election to Labour's Helen Clark, which makes Jenni Shipley the only one of the leaders under discussion here to be followed directly by another female: she had convinced New Zealanders that a woman can lead a government as well as any man.

Angela Dorothea Kasner (1954–) was born in Hamburg but spent most of her youth in the then German Democratic Republic when her father, a Lutheran pastor, was transferred to Brandenburg. She studied physics at the University of Leipzig where she met her husband Ulrich Merkel. **Angela Merkel** spent the next 12 years at the Central Institute for

Physical Chemistry of the Academy of Sciences in Berlin–Adlershof. Only then did her thoughts turn to politics. In the first general election after unification in 1990 she entered the Bundestag (parliament) as member for Stralsund and surrounding districts in east **Germany**, which she has represented ever since. The following year Chancellor Helmut Kohl appointed Merkel as his Minister for Women and Youth, and in 1994 as Minister for the Environment, Nature Conservation and Nuclear Safety. In this role the youngest member of Kohl's cabinet wrote a seminal article on 'The role of science in sustainable development'. We owe the only three scientifically trained and female leaders (Thatcher, Brundtland and Merkel) the fact that the world is finally coming to grips with climate change. Kohl lost the 1998 election and Merkel became leader of the Christian Democratic Union (CDU). In opposition together with the Christian Social Union (CSU), Merkel managed to defeat Gerhard Schröder's Social Democratic Party-led government in **2005**. She was now Germany's first female **chancellor** (head of government).

German author Matthias Krauss has analysed the media's initial assessment of Merkel. *Der Stern* called her 'a physicist with power', while *Die Wirtschaftswoche* considered her to be 'a restless elementary particle' [15]. The qualities that have led to Angela Merkel's early achievements have been evaluated by political scientist Gerd Langguth in the form of 12 interrelated 'theses'. These include 'the ideology-free scientist Merkel as a generalist without a fixation on history … her political viewpoint is formed from the rationality of a scientist'; 'her perception of women in continuously male-dominated politics is relentless and without reservation'; 'her pragmatic outlook towards politics makes ruling with various coalitions possible … She can win or lose all. So far she has won all' [16]. Merkel's pragmatism lost out momentarily to her humanity in 2015 when she opened Germany's borders to all potential refugees, and they came. But her popularity recovered. She has won every election — all in coalition with other parties — from 2005 on. She has made it clear that she will not contest the election in September 2021. Her legacy can be assessed by the recognition she has received internationally. *Forbes* magazine rated her top of the World's 100 Most Powerful Women in virtually every year between 2016 and 2020, as well as the most powerful person in 2012. She has received the highest honours from 13 foreign countries and honorary degrees from ten leading universities around the world.

Maps of Africa around 1900 show only two countries that were not colonised by Europeans: Ethiopia and **Liberia**. Yet Liberia *had* been colonised, though not by Europeans. In 1847 Liberia received its independence from the American Colonisation Society that had governed it since 1821. Emancipated Afro-Americans were encouraged to settle in the country. The fact that most came originally from elsewhere in West Africa, had no tribal connections with the indigenous people and did not speak any of their languages, was of little concern. Naturally the natives resented the newcomers, who largely ignored them and set up a government based on that in the USA. Most native Liberians (who still make up the bulk of the population) lived in the bush, while the Americo-Liberians settled in the capital Monrovia which they rebuilt.

Ellen Johnson Sirleaf (1938–) is the daughter of indigenous parents (a Gola father and Kru mother whose father was German). She married James Sirleaf after graduating from High School. Together they went to the USA on scholarships to study in Madison, Wisconsin: James read agriculture at the University of Wisconsin, Ellen enrolled at Madison Business College. On return they retrieved their three children who had been placed with relatives, but the marriage was faltering and they divorced. Ellen began to work at the Treasury, and in 1969 represented her department at a conference in Monrovia, organised by the Harvard Institute for International Development. Aware of how badly the economy was performing, she did not mince her words. 'I suggested it had something to do with government corruption and our system of kleptocracy. There was only so much one could steal from an economy and expect the economy to keep prospering' [17]. A Harvard professor, one of the organisers, praised her speech but suggested she might consider leaving the country for a while. At once. So began a long period during which Ellen became a critic of the government without also becoming a victim.

After a year at Harvard she was offered the post of deputy minister in the department of finance and returned to Liberia. It began to occur to

Ellen that she was being sidelined here and decided to leave. The contacts she had developed as deputy finance minister enabled her to be offered a job as loan officer at the World Bank. In 1973 she set up home, with her mother and son Rob, in Alexandria, Virginia. Her first posting was to the Latin American and Caribbean division, stationed in Barbados, then to the Eastern African division where she made contacts that would prove useful for the rest of her life. In 1979 she was back in Monrovia as Finance Minister. The following year, after another spate of bad economic news, a native Krahn named Samuel K Doe, a Master Sergeant — soon General — initiated a coup and installed himself as president of Liberia (after murdering President William Tolbert). Ellen managed to explain the recent budget to him without raising his ire. Invited to Philadelphia to give the keynote speech to a group calling itself the Union of Liberian Associations in the Americas, she said '…and then I look at the many idiots in whose hands our nation's fate and progress have been placed, and I simply shake at the unnecessary and tremendous cost which we pay under the disguise of righting the wrongs of the past'. Back in Monrovia she was summoned by the president. '"Oh you think we are idiots!" yelled Doe' [18]. Ellen spent the next year or so in and out of fetid prisons on trumped-up charges, never sure whether she would join the many others who were summarily shot on Doe's orders. Doe had actually wanted her back in government as a senator, but her refusal to do so, especially after he was formally elected president after a rigged election in 1986, continued to enrage him. When she was warned by one of Doe's inner circle that her life was now in great danger she took heed. She decided that the day of her eldest son's wedding would be optimal as the authorities would not be watching out for her so closely. Disguised behind dark glasses she and a friend drove 90 miles southeast of Monrovia to an airstrip where a small privately hired plane was waiting to take them across the border into Côte d'Ivoire. Two days later she was in New York. Her political ambitions had been thwarted but at least she was alive.

For the next ten years Ellen would engage in international missions and conferences on behalf of the United Nations Development Programme across West Africa without returning to Liberia. A new upstart had arrived to terrorise the good people of Liberia. He was Charles Taylor, who in 2012 would be found guilty by a Special Court for Sierra Leone held at the International Criminal Court in The Hague, of war crimes and crimes against humanity and sentenced to 50 years in prison. But in 1997 Ellen was back in Monrovia to contest the presidential election. She had earlier backed Taylor against Doe (who was subsequently tortured and then murdered by Prince Yormie Johnson — no relation, and no prince — another murderous warlord on the streets of Monrovia). She lost to Taylor in what was a fraudulent election and left the country. Under pressure from the US and the international community to resign, Taylor went into exile in Nigeria in 2003. An interim government took over, prior to a presidential election in 2005. This Ellen won and on 16 January **2006** was inaugurated as **president** of Liberia. She was the first woman in the whole of Africa to hold that post. Over the following 12 years — she won the presidential election in 2011 — Ellen successfully steered the war-ravaged country back towards normality. It was an enormous challenge. 'In the chaos of war, our HIV rate had quadrupled. Our children were dying of curable diseases such as tuberculosis, dysentery, measles, malaria, parasites, and malnutrition. Our schools — those that remained — lacked books, equipment, and most critically, teachers. Our clinics and hospitals — those that remained — lacked doctors, nurses, and supplies. The telecommunications age had passed us by. We had a $4.7 billion international debt …'. But her experience of politics (and remaining alive) over three decades served her well. When she decided to step down in 2018, she had achieved an almost impossible improvement in people's lives. 'People sometimes like to ask whether I would have accomplished more or less as a man. I don't have to hesitate to answer that one — I would have accomplished far, far less. I would have been, really, just another man. I think that as a woman I was an exception, and being an exception gave me both the visibility and the drive to succeed. I was ahead of my time, but I am no longer alone. We are breaking barriers daily; in another decade there will be hundreds of women in real positions of leadership all over Africa and all over the world' [19].

Republicanism is not the enemy of androcentrism. Neither the USA nor France have yet elected a female leader, though they have had 250 years to think about it. Nor for that matter have the Swiss. We are unlikely to see a female general secretary of the Chinese Communist Party, or a female president of Russia, in the near future. The culturally androcentric country of Japan may witness an empress before a female premier. But the USA, which came close to a female president in 2016 (and had already seen a female Leader in the House of Representatives a decade earlier), will surely elect one in the near future.

Higher Education

For women who wanted to pursue careers in medicine or the humanities, Italy was the place. I have already mentioned the 11th-century school of medicine in Salerno (chapter 5) and the Bologna Academy of Sciences (chapter 6). In fact the University of Bologna awarded its first degree to a woman (in law) in 1237. Two years later the recipient went on to become the university's first female teacher. The continent of Europe continued to be far ahead of Britain or the United States for centuries. Not surprising, when in 1904 a respected scientist, Henry Armstrong, could argue that because women were thought to be lower down the evolutionary scale, 'education can do little to modify her nature' [20]. The first observation is nonsense but the second has a grain of truth in it: one's IQ, whether female or male, changes very little throughout life.

Irish universities (then within the UK) were admitting women to study medicine from the 1880s onwards. The Sorbonne in Paris, too, admitted women to read medicine from 1869 onwards. One to take advantage of this was Elizabeth Garrett, who had learned French in order to enable her to attend the Sorbonne. Back in England, she became 'the first and only female member of the British Medical Association, which promptly followed precedent and prevented any other women from joining' [21]. Garrett went on to found her own hospital for women (her father was a wealthy man who believed in his daughter's ambitions) that became known as the Elizabeth Garrett Anderson Hospital (she had married James

Anderson in 1871) after her death in 1917. Here she spent the best part of her life, teaching female students and specialising in gynaecology. The hospital — which became the Royal Free Hospital — is now part of University College London.

The United States were ahead of Britain in regard to medical education and practise for women. Again, it was a woman of courage and determination who 'dared to kick down the door of the all-male US medical establishment' [22]. But Elizabeth Blackwell, born in England in 1821, did not have a wealthy father. Instead, she and her eight impoverished siblings managed to reach the United States in 1832. 'Within a few years the children were fatherless and penniless, having to earn their own living'. Elizabeth survived by working as a schoolteacher. In 1847 she gained admittance to Geneva Medical College in New York State 'at the discretion of the other students — all male. They voted her in as a prank, but she won them over, finishing top of her class and receiving applause at her graduation'. Unable to qualify as a physician in the USA, Elizabeth went to Paris as a student midwife to gain the necessary experience in obstetrics. In 1857 she and her younger sister Emily, who had managed to obtain a medical degree from Cleveland Medical College, founded the New York Infirmary for Indigent Women and Children. It was an upward struggle. As in Britain, 'when a door opened, it did so solely for an individual woman or owing to a loophole, promptly shutting again; each hard-won victory was for a special case. Women as a whole were still viewed as completely unsuited to the medical profession' [23].

Lady Margaret Hall had been Oxford's first female college (founded 1878), but women had to wait until 1920 to receive a degree from the university. Cambridge University saw its first female college (Girton) founded in 1869, but did not grant female students its degrees until 1948. Radcliffe College in the USA, founded 1894, had close relations with Harvard University over a century but not until 1999 did the two officially merge. In fairness to Harvard, its Medical School admitted women in 1945 (half a century after Johns Hopkins in Baltimore and Cornell in New York City) and its Law School in 1950. When I was a post-doctoral fellow at Yale University Medical School in 1959, none of the female faculty was a graduate of the university. Yale admitted women to full membership only in 1961. Of course there were all-female liberal arts colleges across the United States. The Seven Sisters colleges (Barnard, Bryn Mawr, Mount Holyoke, Radcliffe, Smith, Vassar and Wellesley) founded during the 19th century are an example, but none was a university with research facilities. To recapitulate, women had been able to study medicine in Britain and the USA since the second half of the 19th century, but only in all-female institutions.

My point is simple. Women, generally of the educated class, have been writers for 1,000 years, artists and scientists since the 17th century. But not until the second half of the 20th century did women begin to achieve equality with men in regard to politics or academia. The world of business caught up somewhat later. Yet even as recently as 2017, Mary Beard noted 'just how deeply embedded in Western culture are the mechanisms that silence women, that refuse to take them seriously, and that sever them … from the centres of power' [24].

Like a forest fire that continues to smoulder in parts when most has died down, androcentrism endures in Islamic countries. In Pakistan, 15-year-old Malala Yousafzai was shot by a Taliban gunman in 2003 for wanting an education like that given to boys. Fortunately she survived and 11 years later became the youngest recipient of the Nobel Peace Prize. In neighbouring Afghanistan, Taliban and other Islamic groups shoot women at will, for no reason other than trying to lead a professional life considered normal in the rest of the world. In 2004 the Iranian authorities sentenced a 16-year-old girl to death for premarital sex [25]. The author of that observation, Iranian lawyer Shirin Ebadi, was continuously threatened with death for defending women on trumped-up charges, and for winning the Nobel Peace Prize, which enabled her to serve 'the interests of foreign imperialists who seek to weaken Iran' [26].

In the early 1980s I was talking to the wife of my host in Istanbul [27], who mentioned that, to her disappointment, the head scarf was returning among the female students. A prophetic remark. President Recep Tayyid Erdogan is in the process of reversing most of the innovative reforms that his predecessor President Kemal Atatürk had introduced during the 1920s and 30s in an attempt to turn the decadent Islamic country into a modern secular democracy. As I write, Princess Latifa, daughter of Sheikh Mohammed bin Rashid Al Maktoum, prime minister of the United Arab Emirates, is being held prisoner in Dubai by her father. Her crime? Trying to escape his clutches in 2018 in order to lead an independent life. A few years earlier Latifa's elder sister Shamsa had managed to get to England but she, too, was eventually abducted and returned to captivity. In medieval times Islam was a beacon of culture and learning. The rise of Wahhabism during the 18th century contributed to the decline of these values. Malign influences continue to prevent a resurgence of female tolerance today.

Notes

1. see https://richardlangworth.com/fake-quotes-astor
2. from *The World in 2030 AD*, quoted by Rees (2018), p 12.
3. Roberts (2019), p 956.
4. Fara (2018), p 15.
5. see https://guides.library.harvard.edu/c.php?g=357201&p=2468919
6. probably on account of Operation Blue Star in June of 1984, ordered by Gandhi in order to capture the insurgent Sikh leader Jamail Singh Bhindranwale and his followers who were hiding inside the Golden Temple complex in Amritsar.
7. she shortened her surname from Meyerson in 1956 when she was appointed Foreign Minister. All officials travelling abroad were asked to adopt a Hebrew name and Golda chose Meir, meaning 'illuminate'.
8. quoted by Pasternak (2012), p 132.
9. both *ibid*, p 134.
10. Carol Bellamy, Director-General of UNICEF; Catherine Bertini, chair of the UN Standing Committee on Nutrition; Gro Harlem Brundtland, Director-General of WHO; Mary Robinson, High Commissioner for Human Rights; Dr Nafis Sadik, leader of the World Population Fund.
11. Brundtland (2002), p 147.
12. *ibid*, p 84.
13. *ibid*, p 154.

14. *Reconciliation: Islam, Democracy and the West* (New York City: Harper Collins, 2008) published posthumously.

15. Krauss (2005), pp 171–172; my translation quoted in Pasternak (2012), p 142.

16. Langguth (2008), pp 391–424; my translation quoted in Pasternak (2012), p 142.

17. Sirleaf (2009), p 55.

18. *ibid*, pp 122 and 124.

19. *ibid*, pp 276 and 315.

20. Fara (2018), footnote on p 35.

21. Heffer (2013), p 558.

22. Hannah Wunsch, reviewing Janice P Nimura: *The Doctors Blackwell: How Two Pioneering Sisters Brought Medicine to Women and Women to Medicine* (New York and London: W W Norton, 2021) in *Nature* **589**: 192–193 (2021)

23. all quotations, *ibid*.

24. Beard (2017), p x.

25. Ebadi (2016), p xii.

26. *ibid*, p 163.

27. *Introduction to Human Biochemistry* (1979) had been translated into Turkish and my editor at the Oxford University Press told me that instead of royalties the authorities were offering me and my wife a tour of the country with a few lectures thrown in: I accepted. Dr Kaya Emerk was professor of biochemistry and his wife taught English in the building at Uskudar (Scutari), where Florence Nightingale had once tended soldiers injured in the Crimean War.

Chapter 8

Primitive Societies in Modern Times

The main theme of this book is that androcentrism is mainly a cultural phenomenon, what Richard Dawkins might describe as a 'meme' [1]. It began to develop out of pastoralism from around 8000 BCE onwards, becoming established by the beginning of the Bronze Age *c* 3000 BCE. The earliest civilisations, in Mesopotamia and Egypt, were distinctly androcentric; those along the Indus Valley and in Persia, less so. In corners of the world that were left untouched by civilisation, the relative gender neutrality — or matriarchy in some cases — of the Palaeolithic Age presumably endured. We cannot be sure, for there are no written records and few archaeological clues (I mentioned the Le Vigneau community in chapter 2). But in areas like the savanna of east Africa and the desert of southern Africa, indigenous tribes have maintained largely independent lives well into the 20th century. Elsewhere, in the Americas and Australia, Europeans did make contact but left (or forced) the indigenous inhabitants to live in separate areas. The extent to which such different communities displayed an androcentric way of life is what this chapter aims to explore.

Many primitive societies today are matrilineal (descent through the mother) and matrilocal (the wife rules the roost and the husband moves into her house on marriage). Matriliny is common among developed African nations, though they are firmly patriarchal. Judaism is the prime example of matriliny and androcentrism: 'Thank you, God, for not making me a woman'. Catherine Gasquoine Hartley, writing in 1914, makes a detailed case for reconciling 'the theory of mother-right' with 'the patriarchal family' [2].

Anthropologist Christopher Boehm addresses a different but related question. Why are most of the primitive communities egalitarian? This, you might think, is the 'default' situation. But Boehm considers that an active opposition to chiefdom underlies egalitarian outcomes when the group size is relatively small — between a few dozen and a few hundred individuals. He proposes eight types of sanction, any one of which is evident in some 50 primitive groups around the world. These range from public opinion and criticism, through ridicule and disobedience, all the way to execution [3]. Without chiefs to lead them, wars among such primitive groups are unlikely. Did the rejection of one hierarchy (chiefdom) also lead to the repudiation of another (male supremacy)? Recall that the emergence of chiefs among the cattle-herding people of the Pontic-Caspian region (chapter 2) was one of the triggers for the development of androcentrism. Males were naturally considered superior to females as enforcers of rules: their physical strength versus women's empathy.

At the end of the 20th century there were about five million persons described as 'Indigenous Peoples Who Are or Were Hunter-Gatherers' in the world. Of these, two million are in India and the Andaman Islands, 600,000 in Southeast Asia (mainly Malaysia), 450,000 in Africa (mainly central and southern Africa), 300,000 in Australia, 200,000 in Siberia and the Russian Far East, 150,000 in North America (US and Canada), 100,000 in the North Polar region (Russia, Greenland, US and Canada), 26,000 in East Asia (mainly Japan) and 3,500 in Latin America (mainly Ecuador, Venezuela, Colombia, Paraguay and Bolivia) [4]. It is difficult, if not impossible, to generalise about the precise gender relations of so many diverse tribes and smaller bands living in regions that vary from the icy to the equatorial.

A measure of the type of life led by such different societies was introduced in 1980. Known as the 'Cultural Complexity of the 186 Societies in the Standard Cross-Cultural Sample', it uses criteria such as writing, fixity of residence, agriculture, urbanisation, technological socialisation, land transport, money, density of population, political integration, social stratification and mode of subsistence to come up with a list of complexities, ranging from 0 to 40 [5]. At 0, for example, are the Hadza of Tanzania and the Mbuti pygmies of the Democratic Republic of Congo; at 1 are the Botocudo and Aweikoma from Brazil and the Yahgan from Tierra del Fuego; at 2 are the !Kung or San Khoisian speakers from the Kalahari, as well as the Semang (a Negroid group of the Malay Peninsula) and the Tiwi from islands off Australia's Northern Territory. All these are considered 'foragers'. At the other end are groups like the Aztecs at 34, the Khmer at 36, the (ancient) Egyptians at 37, Balinese at 38, Babylonians and Romans at 39, and (presumably also ancient) Siamese, Chinese and Japanese at 40.

Everyone's lineage, of course, starts in Africa. I will begin by describing two peoples who never left that continent: the San or Bushmen of the Kalahari (that include the !Kung), and the Hadza of Tanzania. Of those who migrated to Eurasia, the Semang and other Malayan Aboriginals are still there: their story will be told next. I will end with the descendants of two migratory waves out of Eurasia. First, those who by 50,000 years ago had reached Papua New Guinea across open water from Southeast Asia, namely the ancestors of the Aborigines of Australia and the Trobriand Islanders. Second, the intrepid people of the Siberian steppe who migrated eastward across the then-land bridge into Alaska more than 15,000 years ago. They went on to populate North and South America and are generally described as Native Americans.

The Bushmen of the Kalahari

These people, also known as San (meaning forager), have lived in their present location for more than 25,000 — maybe even 50,000 — years. Today there are more than 90,000 Bushmen, of whom around 50,000 live in Botswana, 30,000 in Namibia, with the remainder in South Africa, Angola and Zimbabwe. They occupy the most arid regions of these countries, and even in Botswana account for less than 4% of the population. The majority, as elsewhere in Southern Africa, are Bantu who did not arrive until the 12th century CE. Bushmen are ethnically one of the most diverse groups of people on Earth. They speak a number of different languages which are as different as, for example, the Indo-European languages (see Figure 3.2) are from Semitic or Chinese. Bushmen still hunt and gather — the former carried out mainly by men, the latter by women — though hunting has largely been replaced by herding, and gathering by farming. They are rated as 2 in the Cultural Complexity index mentioned above.

An illustration of the attitude of Bushmen towards their neighbours has been revealed by a study, carried out between the late 1960s and 2010, of the village of Tsumkwe in Namibia near the border with Botswana. The Bushmen lived in a number of waterholes in the vicinity of the village. This provided them with schooling, health services and shops where they could purchase food and other products. About a third of the Bushmen lived mainly off wild foods (foraged or grown), a third off food mainly bought in the village, and the rest equally on both. 'More interestingly, in 1968–1969, just over half (50.8%) said they liked living in the bush, and most of the rest said they did not. In 2010, 96.9% preferred the bush. Their reasons were equally interesting. Food was more plentiful in the bush than in a town. The bush was quieter, and town was full of alcohol-related bickering. Town life was boring and at the same time stressful, whereas the bush was the place of cultural tradition, "what we are as a people".... They are a contradiction: they retain values of personal liberty, gender equality and a reverence for "the bush". They value both the healing dance and their newfound Christian ideology' [6], (which some readers might not find so contradictory).

Although Bushmen, as mentioned, are an extremely diverse group of people, they share certain characteristics. These include 'small group size', 'detailed knowledge of the environment', 'medicine dance', 'common folklore', 'knowledge of the spirit world' and so forth down to 'flexibility in almost everything'. From the point of view of this book the most significant, of course, is 'egalitarian social structure' [7]. Are the lives of Bushmen likely to change in the future? Not according to one member of the Ju/'hoan tribe who, when interviewed in 2018, said, 'I don't want our culture to change. I want the children to know both: they must know how to read and write. And at the same time, they must also know how to hunt and how to gather' [8].

The Hadza of Tanzania

The Hadza, who currently number around 1,000 people, occupy an area of approximately 4,000 km^2 in northern Tanzania that is halfway between Lake Victoria and the Indian Ocean. Their territory lies above 1,000 m and includes Lake Eyasi that encompasses about a third of their land. Most Hadza live to the south and east of the lake. Half of these still live entirely by hunting and gathering wild plants. Over the past century anthropologists have observed [9] the game to include birds and small mammals, antelope, gazelle, gnu, giraffe, hartebeest, ostrich and zebra, as well as elephant, hippopotamus, rhinoceros and even leopards and lions, though in the latter case the hunter sometimes becomes the prey. Many different kinds of fish are taken from Lake Eyasi. The plants include baobab, berries and other fruit, tubers and roots. Honey, which provides a significant proportion of the Hadza's caloric intake, is a particular delicacy. The other half of the population combine foraging with activities such as acting as game ranger for the Tanzanian government or as guardians of their non-Hadza neighbours' maize fields. No Hadza appears to act as pastoralist or farmer. Not surprisingly they are listed as 0 on the Cultural Complexity index.

Most Hadza live in small camps comprising two or three families. Some are home to no more than a few individuals, others as many as 100. Camps are moved from time to time, depending on the supply of food as well as on seasonal variation. The availability of water, of course, is crucial. Camps are sited sufficiently away from water holes in order for animals (that will provide sustenance) not to be discouraged from using them. Any decision to move is a joint one, with women, who know when foraging sites become depleted, having as much say as the men. Chiefs, as well as shamans, are unknown. Traditionally men hunt, with bow and arrow — often poisoned — as well as with stones and other simple weapons. Women forage in groups; men, generally on their own, also forage. In camp, the sexes converse and eat together.

An example of gender equality among the Hadza is revealed when a Hadza women moves away to marry and mate with a non-Hadza man. 'Very often, however, the woman eventually leaves her husband and returns to raise the child in a Hadza camp. This seems to be because Hadza women are too independent to put up with the sort of treatment they get from non-Hadza men. Hadza women have a good deal of independence and often speak their minds. But with non-Hadza men, they are looked down on, given orders, and more often beaten, so they want to leave and return to a Hadza camp' [10]. No stigma is attached to the returning woman or her child.

The future for the Hadze does not bode well. They may still be 'very different from almost all other populations in the world today' [11], but their lifestyle is threatened by neighbouring groups who are destroying the forests to grow maize. Others are snaring wildlife in order to raise cattle. Tourists now come to photograph people who have so far been resistant to change. But the foreigners are eradicating the very objectives of their visit. For the money that the tourists spend with the Hadza is soon exchanged by neighbouring entrepreneurs for alcohol which is destroying Hadza life. Yet the tourists keep coming. In just 15 years, from 1995 to 2010, their number has risen more than ten-fold.

The Aborigines of the Malay Peninsula

Homo sapiens probably entered the Malay Peninsula around 40,000 years ago. The earliest identifiable inhabitants have been called Negritos [12] and they occupy not just the Malay Peninsula, but most of Southeast Asia (including southern Thailand) as far west as the Andaman Islands. The Negritos of the Malay Peninsula, referred to as Semang, are part of the larger group of indigenous inhabitants known as Orang Asli, meaning 'first people'. These now number around 200,000, or less than 1% of the inhabitants of the Malay Peninsula. Note that the nation of Malaysia includes the states of Sarawak and Sabah along the northern coast of the island of Borneo; some 80% of Malaysians live on the peninsula.

At the end of the 19th century Britain took control of the Federated Malay States (FMS) that encompassed much of the Malay Peninsula. George Alexander de Chazal de Moubray, a District Officer during the early years of the 20th century, has made a detailed study of life before British rule. 'The population consisted exclusively of peasants following matriarchal custom' [13]. Property and land were owned entirely by women. Single men were provided for by their mother or sister, married men by their wife. Men worked on the family property and in exchange received sustenance and their clothes. On the death of a married woman, the property passed not to her husband but to her mother or sisters. Women often married men from outside her tribe. The husband would then become a member of his wife's tribe. If the groom happens to be chief of another tribe, he still becomes a member of his wife's tribe, though his office remains with his original tribe.

I have mentioned (male) chiefs. In addition, each of the four FMS, namely Selangor, Perak, Negeri Sembilan and Pahang, was ruled by a Sultan. The Sunni branch of the Islamic religion had been introduced by traders from Arabia and elsewhere prior to the 12th century. By the 15th century Islam was the national religion, which is still followed by some 60% of the population today. Matriarchy may have declined to the point of its replacement by patriarchy during the 20th century, but in earlier times it co-existed with Islam. Muslims lived in matriarchal societies not just in Malaya but in Sumatra (whence indigenous Malayans came), southern India, and beyond. Vestiges of matriarchal principles survive there to this day, despite being in contradiction with Sharia law. So far as the male rulers of the FMS are concerned, their foremost subordinates were women.

Matriarchy in the Malay Peninsula was still very much in force under British rule 90 years ago. George de Moubray was in no doubt about its social efficacy when he wrote that 'I do not know whether it is universal that the men of races following matriarchal custom are a particularly fine body, but this I do know, that the men of the matriarchal races with which I am familiar ... do stand out from their neighbours'. De Moubray goes on to quote a big-game hunter who was of the opinion that the Negeri Sembilan Malays 'are the finest in the peninsula ... and that they are directly due to matriarchy'. Why should matriarchy work so well?

De Moubray's suggestion is that 'it breeds a spirit of adventure ... the possession of land by the women drives a large proportion of the young men of Negri Sembilan to seek a fortune outside the country. They return to it later with an assured economic position ...' [14].

Australian Aborigines

The first Australians had wandered from Papua New Guinea into northern Australia, then linked by land, more than 50,000 years ago. As they spread over the entire continent during the following thousands of years, they split into many culturally different bands. This makes generalisations difficult. Moreover, our knowledge of the lives led by these people is dependent on the differing views of anthropologists who studied them over a period of more than 100 years. The earliest Europeans to settle in Australia, at Sidney Cove, arrived during the late 18th and early 19th century. Following their appearance the Aboriginal population with whom they made contact declined by up to 90%. This was due in part to the transmission of diseases to which the indigenous people had no immunity, in part to direct conflict. The newcomers were mainly prison warders and their convict charges. These men and their immediate descendants were enured to androcentrism. Not unexpectedly they interpreted some of the feasts and religious ceremonies among the Aboriginals as exhibiting male dominance. What needs to be taken seriously is that the eminent anthropologist Bronislaw Malinowski was 'unequivocal in his conclusion that "the husband had a well nigh complete authority over his wife"' [15], though he also considered that women were generally well treated [16].

Robert Tonkinson, Professor of Anthropology at the University of Western Australia, points out that 'Aboriginal Australia was perhaps unique in the extent to which kinship pervaded ... Life was lived in small, mobile bands of people either closely related, or at least very well known, to one another, so at this social level the need or occasion to give expression to hierarchical distinctions was minimal' [17]. Annette Hamilton, another Australian anthropologist, who has studied the women in the eastern part of the Western Desert, considers that the two sexes lived rather separate lives which gave women a kind of autonomy [18]. A third Australian anthropologist, Diane Bell, conversed with the women of central Australia. She stresses that 'in Aboriginal society, wives were not sold; they were able to exercise a high degree of choice; they fought, they insulted, they remained in their country where their power base was strong. The marriage contract was one between families, it did not entail control over sexuality' [19]. Of course the attitude of the Europeans with whom Aboriginals made contact changed considerably between 1800 and today. The Commonwealth of Australia granted women the vote already in 1902, and they could stand for parliament from that date. So observations of gender relations among Aboriginals during the 20th century may reflect a change towards gender equality resulting from contact with Europeans.

Not all the Aborigines were hunter-gatherers. 'When Major Thomas Mitchell ventured into Australia's inland in the early 1800s … he noted expanses of bright yellow herbs, nine miles of grain-like grass …'. Writer Bruce Pascoe notes that '… when I read these early journals, I came across repeated references to people building dams and wells, planting, irrigating and harvesting seed, preserving the surplus and storing it in houses, sheds or secure vessels … and manipulating the landscape' [20]. Future research may show that these particular tribes should be acknowledged as having begun to practice agriculture independently of outside influence. We should not be too surprised that they established farming practices, for they could be the ancestors of those who remained in Papua New Guinea and went on to develop agriculture 10,000 years ago (see Figure 2.1). Agriculture alone does not necessarily lead to the exploitation of women, especially as these people were not pastoralists (Australia has no indigenous mammals capable of domestication). Only when the group size increases beyond that contained in hamlets or villages do hierarchies with resultant androcentrism arise.

One tribe of Papua New Guineans migrated not south but east to settle among the four islands that together are called Trobriand. Here they now form a community of some 12,000 people.

Trobriand Islanders

The inhabitants of these islands, who score 16 out of 40 in the Culture Complexity index (see above), were probably first visited by a European in 1904. He was Dr Charles Seligman, who was followed by his pupil at the London School of Economics, Bronislaw Malinowski. Malinowski spent two years, between 1915 and 1918, researching the lives of the Trobriand Islanders [21]. He realised early on that the islanders considered descent through the female line to be of prime importance. 'The myth of first emergence is definitely a matrilineal one. It always refers to a women, at times accompanied by a man who is her brother not her husband' [22]. That does not, of course, imply any kind of matriarchy. As mentioned, many African tribes value matrilineal descent while being — since the days of empire in west Africa — entirely patriarchal. But Malinowski did consider the Trobrianders to have been originally matriarchal, though as pointed out in 1931 by George de Moubray (see above) 'the Trobriand system is in such an advanced state of decay that it is on the verge of swinging over into patriarchy; it is only matriliny that holds it back' [23].

An extensive study of Trobriand Islanders living in Kwaibwaga, a village of 300 inhabitants on the island of Kiriwina (population approximately 10,000), was undertaken by Annette Weiner. She made two field trips there during the early 1970s as part of her doctoral thesis at Bryn Mawr College, USA. Fishing and growing food are the main pursuits of the Trobriand Islanders. Yams, which are also exchanged as gifts in marriage and funerary ceremonies, are the main crop in the gardens that are part of each village. Beans, cassava, squash, sweet potato and taro are also grown. The gardens are tended by both sexes, though some sweet potato plots are the preserve of women alone. Weiner notes that 'Kiriwana women play a valuable economic role and they remain decision makers in their own right. ... Men acknowledge the fact that women and girls are the ones to choose a partner, and women have great autonomy in this direction'. Moreover, 'even when a chief wants to marry a beautiful young girl', at least on Kiriwana, 'there is no way she can be forced to go and live with him. A woman defies a chief in the same way that she has the option to reject any man. In sexual affairs and marriage, women have a great degree of autonomy' [24].

The Hopi of North America

Native Americans throughout the continent have been in contact with Europeans for more than 400 years. The result has been disastrous for them. Infectious diseases to which they had no immunity (causing an epidemic of smallpox in 1851) and forced abandonment of their lands are but two of the consequences. So it is not surprising that much of their culture has gradually been eroded. One tribe of whom this appears not to be the case are the Hopi of northeast Arizona, who number almost 20,000 today.

They have lived in houses clinging to the sides of canyons within villages called pueblos by the invading Spanish in the 16th century. Subsistence farming has been their way of life right up to the 1920s. According to Edward Dozier, Native Americans' first academic anthropologist, 'probably all of the structures now found in the Pueblos existed in prehistoric times' [25]. The structures to which he refers are a matrilineal system and strong religious beliefs: 'a Hopi individual's primary rights, duties, responsibilities, and loyalties were to members of his or her household and matrilineage' [26].

Writer Diane LeBow has spent time among the Hopi women, listening to their accounts of life in this matrilineal and matrilocal society. As a result she points out that gender roles among the Hopi are egalitarian and that 'the complementarity of the sexes is institutionalized', that 'women's status among the Hopi is respected and substantial' and that 'anthropological literature has tended to ignore or diminish women's political, economic and social roles' because 'male anthropologists consistently underplay the importance, participation, and authority of Hopi women' [27].

Elsewhere

The foregoing is by no means a comprehensive account of primitive societies in which some form of gender neutrality is exhibited today. In a lecture delivered in 1955, E E Evans-Pritchard quoted fellow anthropologist Robert Lowie in regard to the Crow people who used to live along the Yellowstone River valley but were corralled into south Montana during the

19th century. 'Women were emphatically not chattels ... altogether the position of woman was far from unfavourable ... there were very few feminine disabilities in religious matters ... socially, the women enjoyed a good deal of freedom ... altogether Crow women had a secure place in the tribal life and a fair share in its compensations' [28].

Most societies in rural Africa today are distinctly patriarchal. Yet in some instances women have managed to uphold certain rights and these may well date back to earlier times. The nomadic Fulani living around the Niger in West Africa 60 years ago are an example. Among those whose livelihood depends on sheep, 'priority is given to female heirs in the direct line (daughters, sisters) over male collaterals (brothers, nephews, parallel cousins). An only daughter inherits the whole flock ...' [29]. Another example of societal values in the 1960s is provided by the women of Burundi, a country of strong patriarchal and patrilineal mores. 'The social division of labour assigns to women nearly total responsibility for anything that is related to food, small children and the house. ... a Rundikazi [30] is absolute proprietor of the food supply. The land she farms is her husband's. ... However, it is strictly forbidden for men to take so much as a handful of beans, raw or cooked, or a bit of butter without the wife's permission.' [31].

I referred earlier to the problem that over recent decades of contact with their neighbours, some primitive people are becoming more androcentric. Accounts written over a century ago are therefore valuable. Catherine Gasquoine Hartley, whom I mentioned earlier, presents several. Among the Iroquois of eastern Canada and the USA, women and men elected the chief of each clan. Female councillors decided how much land each household should own. This, together with all property, belonged equally to both sexes, but 'each household was directed by the matron who supervised its domestic economy' [32].

The social organisation of the Khasi Hill tribes of northeast India 'presents one of the most perfect examples still surviving of matriarchal institutions carried out with a logic and a thoroughness which, to those accustomed to regard the status and authority of the father as the foundation of society, are exceedingly remarkable. Not only is the mother the head and source and only bond of union of the family, in the most primitive part of the hills ... she is the only owner of real property, and through her alone is inheritance transmitted' [33].

Further north, among the Pani Kotches tribes of Bengal, Hartley finds the women to be 'in a privileged position, due to their greater industrial activity and intelligence', leading to 'an economic matriarchy' [34]. Finally, within the Pelew or Palao, who occupy a small group of islands to the southeast of the Philippines, 'the existence of the clan depends entirely on the life of the women, and not at all on the life of the men. If the women survive, it is no matter though every man in the clan should perish, for the women will, as usual, marry men of another clan, and their offspring will inherit their mother's clan, and thereby prolong its existence' [35].

I rest my case. Primitive man may have been aware of his greater strength, but he seems not to have exercised control over women to the extent that he did from the Age of Bronze onwards. If I were writing this chapter 100 years ago, there would probably have been more examples of matriarchy or gender neutrality among contemporary primitive peoples. 100 years on, there are unlikely to be any (though the books that I have consulted will hopefully still be there). To conclude, androcentrism is predominantly a cultural phenomenon: an episode that has spanned more than five millennia.

Notes

1. Richard Dawkins: *The Selfish Gene* (Oxford: Oxford University Press, new edition 1989), p 192.
2. Hartley (1914), p 19 *et seq.*
3. Christopher Boehm *et al*: Egalitarian behavior and reverse dominance hierarchy. *Current Anthropology* **34**: 227–254 (1993).
4. Robert K Hitchcock and Megan Biesele: *Introduction*, in Schweitzer *et al* (2000), p 5.
5. reproduced in Marlowe (2010), pp 70–71.
6. Barnard (2019), p 132 *et seq.*
7. *ibid*, p 173.

8. quoted by Barnard (2019), p 134.

9. see Marlowe (2010), pp 20–27.

10. *ibid*, p 172.

11. *ibid*, p 286.

12. their dark colour evolved through natural selection over tens of thousands of years in response to the damaging effects of bright sunlight in the region. They are no more related to the peoples of sub-Saharan Africa than, for example, black Ethiopians are. The latter show a closer relationship to Armenians, Jews, and Norwegians than to the Bantu: see James F Wilson *et al*: Population genetic structure of variable drug response. *Nature Genetics* **29**: 265–269 (2001).

13. Moubray (1931), p 19.

14. *ibid*, pp 210–212.

15. in Bronislaw Malinowski: *The Family among the Australian Aborigines* (New York: Schocken Books, 1963, p 84; originally published in London: University of London Press, 1913); quoted by Robert Tonkinson: *Gender Role Transformation among Australian Aborigenes*, in Schweitzer *et al* (2000), p 346.

16. Malinowski (1963), pp 80–88.

17. Robert Tonkinson: *op cit* in Schweitzer *et al* (2000), p 345.

18. Annette Hamilton: Dual social systems: Technology, labour and women's secret rites in the eastern Western Desert. *Oceania* **51**: 4–19 (1980).

19. Diane Bell: *Daughters of the Dreaming* (Sydney: McPhee Gribble/George Allen and Unwin, 1983), p 100.

20. both quotations from: Rethinking indigenous Australia's agricultural past, https://www.abc.net.au/radionational/programs/archived/bushtelegraph/rethinking-indigenous-australias-agricultural-past/5452454; see also Bill Gammage: *The Biggest Estate on Earth: How Aborigines made Australia* (Sydney and London: Allen and Unwin, 2011).

21. although of Polish heritage, Malinowski was a citizen of the Austro-Hungarian Empire. Therefore he could not return to his position at the London School of Economics until the war between Germany and its ally was over.

22. quoted by Weiner (1976), p 37.

23. Moubray (1931), p 51.

24. Weiner (1976), pp 117 and 135 respectively.

25. quoted by Rushforth and Upham (1992), p 21.

26. Rushforth and Upham (1992), p 40.

27. Diane LeBow: *Rethinking Matriliny among the Hopi*, in Ruby Rohrlich and Elaine Hoffman Baruch: *Women in search of Utopia: Mavericks and Mythmakers* (New York: Schocken Books, 1984), pp 8, 9 and 13 respectively.

28. Evans-Pritchard (1965), p 42 *et seq.*

29. Marguerite Dupire: *The Position of Women in a Pastoral Society*, in Paulme (1963), p 90.

30. woman of Burundi.

31. Ethel M Albert: *Women of Burundi: A Study of Social Values*, in Marguerite Dupire: *The Position of Women in a Pastoral Society*, in Paulme (1963), p 199.

32. Hartley (1914), p 106.

33. Hartley (1914), quoting Sir Charles Lyell, the geologist whose proposals on the evolution of the Earth's crust inspired Charles Darwin, p 132.

34. *ibid*, pp 158 and 159.

35. *ibid*, quoting ethnographer John Stanislaw Kubary, p 155.

Epilogue

A few years ago I was discussing the possibility of a book on outstanding women through the ages and across the globe with one of London's leading literary agents. She liked the idea but pointed out that publishers of books on women preferred them to be written by female authors. I was astounded. Had androcentrism been replaced by feminism in the 21st century? In any case, surely a male voice expounding the equality of women is particularly compelling? She compromised by saying that if I was joined by my daughter [1] it might work rather well. As mentioned in the Prologue, it didn't. It has occurred to me that the publisher to whom I first sent a treatment for this book turned it down because I was not female (and I have no plans to remedy this).

The suffragette movement caused politicians and the public to take seriously the views expressed by the likes of Mary Wollstonecraft and Jeremy Bentham at the turn of the 18th century. The result has been the gradual erosion of androcentrism throughout the last century. Much remains to be done to eradicate this disease entirely. Girls and women in certain Muslim countries continue to live in fear for their lives. Yet some of today's feminists seem more concerned about which lavatory a transgender person should enter. When I first visited the United States in 1957 there were three lavatory entrances at Greyhound bus stations in the southern states: 'men', 'women' and 'colored'. We have come a long way.

This narrative has focussed on the rise of androcentrism in Europe and the Near East, followed by its decline. A similar story might be told about China, and it would be interesting for a scholar to do so. Particularly worthwhile would be a study of androcentrism in Africa. The last chapter provided instances of isolated communities who have maintained a 'primitive' way of life to this day. But elsewhere in Africa, great civilisations developed during the past millennium, just as they had done in Eurasia in earlier times. The empires of ancient Ghana [2], Mali and Songhay — not to mention Egypt — contained cities of culture like Timbuktu. In southeast Africa, Great Zimbabwe boasted the largest stone building in the whole of sub-Saharan Africa. The empires in the west all declined, just as those of Mesopotamia did, and for a similar reason: incursions by warring enemies. Like the decay of the Indus Valley civilisation, that of Great Zimbabwe remains a mystery. A comprehensive assessment of the extent to which androcentrism has affected the lives of women throughout the ages in sub-Saharan Africa would surely make a more valuable addition to historiography than some of the proposals currently advocated by zealous academics who seem to have lost sight of the purpose of a university education [3].

Prostitution is said to be the oldest profession in the world. Androcentrism, war and slavery — the last two connected — go back to the same time. In the civilisations [4] of the Bronze Age and the Classical Age they were part of everyday life. Wars are generally fought for possession of land or wealth. Acquisition of booty, in the form of men for labour and women for pleasure, has been another. Civil wars, of which those in the Roman republic were among the first, are fought for political reasons or to overthrow a tyrant.

Slavery, but not androcentrism, had gradually petered out in most of Europe by the time of the Middle Ages. In Russia serfdom continued unchecked. Tsar Alexander II (1818–1881) tried to liberate the serfs and was assassinated for his attempt. Any moves towards emancipation were reversed by his son Alexander III. The story in Africa is rather different. In west Africa the trade in slaves, gold and salt across the Sahara sustained the great empires that grew up around the Niger. The explorer David Livingstone [5] considered the Arab slave trade to Zanzibar off Africa's east coast (abetted by some unscrupulous Africans) that was still at its height in the 1870s to be 'a gross outrage of the common law of mankind' [6]. The Atlantic trade out of west Africa was of course equally pernicious but at least one African nation has apologised for it [7].

In this book I have made several propositions. In chapter one I came to the conclusion that the structure of the brain, like that of liver and heart, kidney and intestine, is gender neutral. Hormones control emotions like aggression or empathy, but do not affect cognitive ability. Females are as clever or as stupid as males, across a wide spectrum. I made the same argument elsewhere in relation to ethnicity: the potential for wisdom or folly is the same in all humans — whether Africans or their European and Asian descendants [8].

If intellectual prowess is the same in both sexes, then the main cause of androcentrism would seem to be cultural, not innate. This proposal rests on the shoulders of others: sociologist Friedrich Engels in the 19th century, ethnologist Claude Lévi-Strauss in the mid-20th century, archaeologist Marija Gimbutas who made ground-breaking discoveries during the 1950s and 60s, historian Gerda Lerner at the end of the 1980s, and neuroscientist Gina Rippon today. Robert Graves, eclectic writer and Professor of Poetry at Oxford University from 1961 to 1966, is another. Thus 'the most important study of all, utterly dwarfing all economic and political ones, is for the changing relationship between men and women down the centuries — from prehistoric times to the present ...'; 'one must think back to the primitive age, when men invariably treated women as the holier sex, since they alone perpetuated the race'; 'a revolution in early historical times that upset the balance between male and female principles, namely, the suppression of matriarchy by patriarchy' and 'patriarchy is, indeed, a phenomenon associated with cattle-owning nomads' [9].

I am aware that my proposal is controversial, and some readers may disagree with my views. But surely John Stuart Mill's remark in 1859, that 'in this age mere example of nonconformity, the mere refusal to bend the knee to custom, is a service' [10] is as valid, if not more so, today. Arguments among scientists and historians, philosophers and sociologists have been the basis of our culture and our knowledge of the world. Stifling debate by diktat from self-appointed warriors of righteousness who wish to revive the Inquisition achieves nothing of value.

Intellectual ability may be gender neutral, but a woman's innate empathy might affect her decisions. Could the carnage caused by two world wars in the last century have been avoided if women had been in charge? A Maria Theresa in 1914 might have been less belligerent than Kaiser Wilhelm II and Emperor Franz Joseph. A Theresa May in 1918 might not have urged the victors to 'squeeze the German nation until the pips squeak' — words uttered by British prime minister Lloyd George that led eventually to political instability in Germany and the rise of fascism. On the other hand Catherine de Medici's actions in 1572 that led to the St Bartholomew Day massacre of Huguenots has shades of Hitler's Kristallnacht against the Jews in 1938. A Margaret Thatcher might not have pursued the appeasement of Hitler as Neville Chamberlain did. But such games are meaningless. The potentiality for cruelty or kindness, stupidity or wisdom, in either sex is so vast that there is no way of predicting what kind of person is thrown up at any point in time.

In 1986 Gerda Lerner wrote: 'The system of patriarchy is a historic construct; it has a beginning; it will have an end. Its time seems to have nearly run its course — it no longer serves the needs of men or women ... What will come after, what kind of structure will be the foundation for alternate forms of social organization we cannot yet know ... But we already know that woman's mind, at last unfettered after so many millennia, will have its share in providing vision, ordering, solutions.' [11].

Notes

1. see www.annapasternak.co.uk
2. not to be confused with modern Ghana, the old Gold Coast, 1,000 km to the south.
3. see, for example, Charles Pasternak: *What is scholarship in the 21ˢᵗ century? The ideas of a university* in Hugo de Burgh, Anna Fazackerley & Jeremy Black (eds): *Can the Prizes still Glitter? The Future of British Universities in a Changing World* (London: University of Buckingham Press, 2007), pp 81–86.
4. I use the term in its original sense of 'a society made up of cities' rather than that of 'a society that is culturally superior to one of uncouth barbarians'. I do not consider androcentrism, war or slavery to be cultured in any way.
5. who thought he had discovered the source of the Nile: that stream was actually the headwater of the Congo, as shown by Livingstone's 'rescuer', Henry

Morton Stanley, who subsequently navigated the river all the way down to its mouth in the Atlantic.

6. explored in Pasternak (2018), p 130.
7. Ghana apologises for its role in slave trade; see https://www.modernghana. com/news/102821/ghana-apologizes-for-its-role-in-slave-trade-coun.html
8. see Pasternak (2018), pp 29–46.
9. from Graves (1965), pp 101, 102, 145 and 146 respectively.
10. quoted by Mervyn Horder in his introduction to Edith Sitwell: *English Eccentrics* (London: The Folio Society, 1994), p x.
11. Lerner (1986), p 229.

Bibliography

Alic, Margaret: *Hypatia's Heritage: A History of Women in Science from Antiquity to the late Nineteenth Century* (London: The Women's Press, 1986)

Anthony, David W: *The Horse, the Wheel, and Language* (Princeton, NJ: Princeton University Press, 2007)

Barnard, Alan: *Bushmen: Kalahari Hunter-Gatherers and Their Descendants* (Cambridge: Cambridge University Press, 2019)

Beard, Mary: *Pompeii: The Life of a Roman Town* (London: Profile Books, 2008)

Beard, Mary: *SPQR: A History of Ancient Rome* (London: Profile Books, 2015)

Beard, Mary: *Women & Power: A Manifesto* (London: Profile Books, 2017)

Beard, Mary: *Civilisations* (London: Profile Books, 2018)

Bond, Alan and Mark Hempsell: *A Sumerian Observation of the Köfels' Impact Event* (London: Alcuin Academics, 2008)

Brooke, John: *Seven Months in Rural Chad* (London: Austin Macauley, 2020)

Brosius, Maria: *Women in Ancient Persia 559–331 BC* (Oxford: Clarendon Press, 1996)

Brundtland, Gro Harlem: *Madam Prime Minister: A Life in Power and Politics* (New York: Farrar, Straus and Giroux, 2002)

Bynum, Caroline Walker: *Jesus as Mother: Studies in the Spirituality of the High Middle Ages* (Berkeley: University of California Press, 1984)

Childe, Vere Gordon: *The Most Ancient Near East* (London: Norton & Company, 1928)

Childe, Vere Gordon: *The Bronze Age* (Cambridge: Cambridge University Press, 1930)

Clark, Gillian: *Women in the Ancient World* (Oxford: Oxford University Press, 1989)

Coles, J M and A F Harding: *The Bronze Age in Europe: An Introduction to the Prehistory of Europe c 2000–700 BC* (London: Methuen & Co Ltd, 1979)

Crankshaw, Edward: *Maria Theresa* (London: Longmans, 1969)

Crawford, Harriet: *The Sumerian World* (London: Routledge, 2013)

Crüsemann, Nicola, Margarete van Ess, Markus Hilgert and Beate Salje (eds): *Uruk: First City of the Ancient World* (translator and ed Timothy Potts; Los Angeles: The J Paul Getty Museum, 2019)

Curry, Andrew: *Göbekli Tepe: The World's First Temple* (Washington, DC: Smithsonian Institute, 2008)

Davies, William and Ruth Charles (eds): *Dorothy Garrod and the Progress of the Palaeolithic* (Oxford: Oxbow, 1999)

Dinshaw, Caroline and David Wallace (eds): *Medieval Women's Writing* (Cambridge: Cambridge University Press, 2003)

Dixon, Simon: *Catherine the Great* (London: Profile Books, 2009)

Donaldson, James: *Woman: Her Position and Influence in Ancient Greece and Rome and among the Early Christians* (London: Longmans, Green and Co, 1907)

Downey, Kirstin: *Isabella: The Warrior Queen* (New York: Doubleday, 2014)

Durkheim, Émile: *The Division of Labor In Society* (2nd revised edition, translator George Simpson; New York: The Free Press, 1964)

Ebadi, Shirin: *Until We Are Free: My Fight for Human Rights in Iran* (London: Rider Books, 2016)

Enders, Clare: *Female Voices* (London: Enders Analysis, 2020). Libraries can acquire a free copy: Contact clareenders@endersanalysis.com

Engels, Frederick: *The Origin of the Family, Private Property and the State* (translator Ernest Untermann; Chicago: Charles H Kerr & Company Co-operative, 1902)

Evans-Pritchard, E E: *The Position of Women in Primitive Societies and Other Essays in Social Anthropology* (London: Faber and Faber, 1965)

Fairweather, Maria: *Madame de Stael* (London: Constable, 2005)

Fara, Patricia: *Pandora's Breeches: Women, Science and Power in the Enlightenment* (London: Pimlico, 2004)

Fara, Patricia: *A Lab of One's Own: Science and Suffrage in the First World War* (Oxford: Oxford University Press, 2018)

Freeman, Philip: *Searching for Sappho: The Lost Songs and World of the First Woman Poet*, (New York City, NY: W. W. Norton & Company, 2016)

Frieda, Leonie: *Catherine de Medici* (London: Phoenix, 2005)

Gimbutas, Marija: *Bronze Age Cultures in Central and Eastern Europe* (The Hague: Mouton & Co, 1965)

Gimbutas, Marija: *Goddesses and Gods of Old Europe, 6500–3500 BC: Myths and Cult Images* (London: Thames and Hudson, 1982)

Graves, Robert: *Mammon and the Black Goddess* (London: Cassell, 1965)

Greene, Ellen (ed): *Women Poets in Ancient Greece and Rome* (Norman: University of Oklahoma Press, 2005)

Hartley, C Gasquoine: *The Position of Woman in Primitive Society: A Study of the Matriarchy* (London: Eveleigh Nash, 1914)

Heffer, Simon: *High Minds: The Victorians and the Birth of Modern Britain* (London: Windmill Books, 2014)

Hingley, Richard and Christina Unwin: *Boudica: Iron Age Warrior Queen* (London: Hambledon and London, 2005)

Holland, Tom: *Persian Fire: The First World Empire and the Battle for the West* (London: Abacus, 2005)

Johnson, Paul: *Elizabeth: A Study in Power and Intellect* (London: Weidenfeld and Nicolson, 1974)

Jones, Michael K and Malcolm G Underwood: *The King's Mother: Lady Margaret Beaufort Countess of Richmond and Derby* (Cambridge: Cambridge University Press, 1992)

Kenoyer, Jonathan Mark: *Ancient Cities of the Indus Valley Civilization* (Oxford: Oxford University Press, 1998)

Knopik, Valerie S, Jenae M Neiderhiser, John C DeFries and Robert Plomin: *Behavioral Genetics* (7th edition; New York: Worth, 2017)

Koch, John T and Barry Cunliffe (eds): *Celtic from the West 2: Rethinking the Bronze Age and the Arrival of Indo-European in Atlantic Europe* (Oxford: Oxbow Books, 2013)

Krauss, Matthias: *Das Mädchen für alles: Angela Merkel — ein Annäherungsversuch* (Anderbeck: Anderbeck Verlag, 2005)

Labarge, Margaret Wade: *Women in Medieval Life: A Small Sound of the Trumpet* (London: Hamish Hamilton, 1986)

Ladizinsky, Gideon: *Plant Evolution Under Domestication* (Dordrecht: Springer, 1998)

Langguth, Gerd: *Angela Merkel: Aufstieg zur Macht. Biografie* (Munich: Deutscher Taschenbuch Verlag, 2008)

Lerner, Gerda: *The Creation of Patriarchy* (Oxford: Oxford University Press, 1986)

Leyser, Henrietta: *Medieval Women: A Social History of Women in England 450–1500* (London: Weidenfeld & Nicolson, 1996)

Loades, David: *Elizabeth I* (London: Hambledon and London, 2003)

Mackay, Robert: *Early Indus Civilizations* (2nd edition, revised and enlarged by Dorothy Mackay; London: Luzac and Co Ltd, 1948)

Maddocks, Fiona: *Hildegard of Bingen: The Woman of Her Age* (London: Headline, 2001)

Marcus, Leah S, Janet Mueller and Mary Beth Rose (eds): *Elizabeth I: Collected Works* (Chicago: University of Chicago Press, 2000)

Marlowe, Frank W: *The Hadza: Hunter-Gatherers of Tanzania* (Berkeley: University of California Press, 2010)

Mazoyer, Marcel and Laurence Roudart: *A History of World Agriculture* (translator James H Membrez; London: Earthscan, 2003)

Meek, Christine and Catherine Lawless (eds): *Studies on Medieval and Early Modern Women 4: Victims or Viragos?* (Dublin: Four Courts Press, 2005)

Mickel, Emanuel J, Jr: *Marie de France* (New York: Twayne, 1974)

Moubray, George Alexander de Chazal: *Matriarchy in the Malay Peninsula and Neighbouring Countries* (London: George Routledge & Sons, 1931)

Nabhan, Gary Paul: *Where Our Food Comes From: Retracing Nicolay Vavilov's Quest to End Famine* (Washington, DC: Island Press, 2009)

Oliver, Neil: *Wisdom of the Ancients: Life Lessons from our Distant Past* (London: Transworld, 2020)

Olson, Linda and Kathryn Kerby-Fulton (eds): *Voices in Dialogue: Reading Women in the Middle Ages* (Notre Dame, IN: University of Notre Dame Press, 2005)

Parker, Matthew: *The Sugar Barons: Family, Corruption, Empire and War* (London: Hutchinson, 2011)

Parsons. Nicholas T: *Vienna: A Cultural and Literary History* (Oxford: Signal Books, 2008)

Pasternak, Charles: *Quest: The Essence of Humanity* (Chichester: Wiley, 2003)

Pasternak, Charles (ed): *What Makes Us Human?* (Oxford: Oneworld, 2007)

Pasternak, Charles: *Blinkers: Scientific Ignorance and Evasion* (Huntingdon, Cambridgeshire: Smith-Gordon, 2012)

Pasternak, Charles: *Africa South of the Sahara: Continued Failure or Delayed Success?* (Bicester, Oxon: Words by Design, 2018)

Paulme, Denise (ed): *Women of Tropical Africa* (translator H M Wright; London: Routledge and Kegan Paul, 1963)

Power, Carla: *If the Oceans Were Ink: An Unlikely Friendship and a Journey to the Heart of the Quran* (New York: Henry Holt and Company, 2015)

Price, T Douglas and Gary M Feinman (eds): *Foundations of Social Inequality* (New York: Plenum Press, 1995)

Pringle, Peter: *The Murder of Nicholai Vavilov: The Story of Stalin's Persecution of One of the Twentieth Century's Greatest Scientists* (London: JR Books, 2009)

Quinn, Susan: *Marie Curie: A Life* (London: Heinemann, 1999)

Redwood, John: *Reason, Ridicule and Religion: The Age of Enlightenment in England 1660–1750* (London: Thames and Hudson, 1976)

Rees, Martin: *On The Future: Prospects for Humanity* (Princeton, NJ: Princeton University Press, 2018)

Renaud, Emma: *Mary Beale (1633–1699): Première Femme Peintre Professionelle en Grande-Bretagne* (Paris: L'Harmattan, 2010)

Rippon, Gina: *Gendered Brain: The New Neuroscience that Shatters the Myth of the Female Brain* (London: The Bodley Head, 2019)

Roberts, Andrew: *Churchill: Walking with Destiny* (London: Penguin Books, 2019)

Robertson, Michael: *The Last Utopians: Four Late Nineteenth Century Visionaries and Their Legacy* (Princeton, NJ: Princeton University Press, 2018)

Robins, Gay: *Women in Ancient Egypt* (London: British Museum Press, 1993)

Robinson, Andrew: *The Indus Lost Civilizations* (London: Reaktion Books, 2015)

Rushforth, Scott and Steadman Upham: *A Hopi Social History: Anthropological Perspectives on Sociocultural Persistence and Change* (Austin, TX: University of Texas Press, 1992)

Saini, Angela: *Inferior: The True Power of Women and the Science that Shows It* (London: Fourth Estate, 2017)

Schweitzer, Peter P, Megan Biesele and Robert K Hitchcock (eds): *Hunters and Gatherers in the Modern World: Conflict, Resistance, and Self-Determination* (New York, NY: Berghahn Books, 2000)

Sirleaf, Ellen Johnson: *This Child will be Great: Memoirs of a Remarkable Life by Africa's First Woman President* (New York: Harper Collins, 2009)

Spencer, Herbert: *Principles of Sociology* (New York: D Appleton and Co, 1912)

Sykes, Rebecca Wragg: *Kindred: Neanderthal Life, Love, Death and Art* (London: Bloomsbury Sigma, 2020)

Tyldesley, Joyce: *Daughters of Isis: Women of Ancient Egypt* (London: Viking, 1994)

Ueki, Masatoshi: *Gender Equality in Buddhism* (New York City, NY: Peter Lang, 2001)

Vavilov, Nikolai I: *Origin and Geography of Cultivated Plants* (translator Doris Löve; Cambridge: Cambridge University Press, 1992)

Watt, Diane (ed): *Medieval Women in their Communities* (Cardiff: University of Wales Press, 1997)

Watts, Edward J: *Hypatia: The Life and Legend of an Ancient Philosopher* (Oxford: Oxford University Press, 2017)

Weiner, Annette B: *Women of Value, Men of Renown: New Perspectives in Trobriand Exchange* (Austin, TX: University of Texas Press, 1976)

Wheeler, Sir Mortimer: *The Indus Civilization* (Supplementary volume to the Cambridge History of India, 3rd edition; Cambridge: Cambridge University Press, 1968)

Wilson, Edward O: *The Origins of Creativity* (London, Allen Lane, 2017)

Winder, Simon: *Lotharingia: A Personal History of Europe's Lost Country* (London: Picador, 2019)

Winsbury, Rex: *Zenobia of Palmyra: History, Myth and the Neo-Classical Imagination* (London: Duckworth, 2010)

Wrangham, Richard: *Catching Fire: How Cooking Made Us Human* (Basic Books, 2009)

Zahran, Yasmine: *Zenobia between Reality and Legend* (BAR International Series 1169, Oxford: Archaeopress, 2003)

Index

Numbers in *italics* refer to notes